starting out in
checkers

RICHARD PASK

Published by Everyman Publishers plc, London

First published 2001 by Everyman Publishers plc, Gloucester Mansions, 140A Shaftesbury Avenue, London WC2H 8HD

British Library Cataloguing-in-Publication Data
A catalogue record for this book is available from the British Library.

ISBN 1 85744 263 6

Distributed in North America by The Globe Pequot Press, P.O Box 480, 246 Goose Lane, Guilford, CT 06437-0480

All other sales enquiries should be directed to Mindsports, Everyman Publishers plc, Gloucester Mansions, 140A Shaftesbury Avenue, London WC2H 8HD. tel: 020 7539 7600 fax: 020 7379 4060
email: dan@everyman.uk.com website: www.everyman.uk.com

To unsung draughts champions past and present

Note: The game of draughts is known in the US as checkers. Throughout this book the word 'draughts' is used where applicable. However, the two games are identical and the words 'draughts' and 'checkers' are interchangeable.

The Everyman Mind Sports series was designed and developed by First Rank Publishing.

Typeset and edited by First Rank Publishing, Brighton
Production by Book Production Services
Printed and bound in Great Britain by The Cromwell Press Ltd., Trowbridge, Wiltshire

Contents

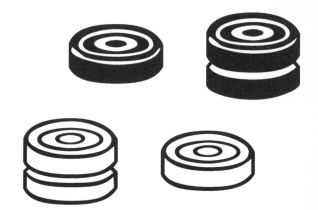

Introduction

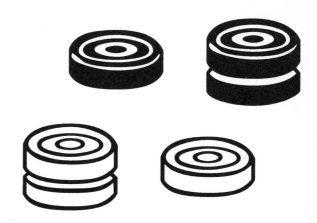

Aims

This book has three main aims:

1) To convince you that draughts, played correctly, is a highly skilful game, abounding in beautiful ideas, which is well worthy of serious attention.

2) To provide a logical, carefully thought out teaching programme, to enable you to attain a competent standard through understanding as opposed to rote learning.

3) To encourage you to delve into more advanced works, to become an active member of one or more of the game's official organisations, and to participate in tournaments and matches.

History

Certain similarities with board games played in earlier ages notwithstanding, draughts was probably invented in the south of France during the 12th century. Of the perhaps mischievous suggestion that it was intended to be a simplified form of chess, one can only say that the inventors got it wrong: not only is draughts profoundly difficult, but it differs from chess in every imaginable way.

English draughts, known as checkers in the USA, is played in every English speaking community in the world, and has boasted a recognised world champion since 1840. It is historically known as the ancient game, and was so named by the French to distinguish it from Spanish, Italian, Polish, Russian, German, Canadian and Turkish draughts, all of which are different games, and each of which has a literature of its own. It stands proudly as one of the world's great games, and is, arguably, the world's most underrated game.

The first book in English on the game was written in 1756, but the real landmarks were Joshua Sturges' *Guide to the Game of Draughts* (1800) and Andrew Anderson's *The Game of Draughts Simplified* (1852). Thereafter, the literature grew apace, with a wealth of material being produced on both sides of the Atlantic, and was, at the turn of the century, supplemented by dozens of newspaper columns, which played an important role in stimulating interest among devotees and recruiting new adherents. To date, well over 1,000 books, pamphlets and journals have been published!

Scottish players dominated the game in its formative years (for a fascinating account see Norrie Reed's *The Scottish School Of Draughts*), culminating in a crushing victory by a Great Britain contingent, led by 5 Scottish grandmasters, over the USA in the 1st International Match of 1905. However, this defeat stung the USA into action, and they have led the way ever since, winning the 2nd (1927), 3rd (1973),

4th (1983), 5th (1989) and 6th (1995) matches by very convincing margins. The 7th match, between the USA and the United Kingdom and Ireland, is scheduled to be played in Morecambe in October 2001, and should prove to be a much closer affair.

Difficulty

In primary education, to 'differentiate' means to meet the needs of all the children, irrespective of their ability. This can either be done by task: giving the more able children harder work, and the less able children easier work; or by outcome: finding a single activity of sufficient scope to allow all of them to succeed at their own level. As an activity permitting differentiation by outcome (for all human beings!), draughts is hard to beat. The problem for enthusiasts is that, while it is universally acknowledged that virtually anyone can understand the rudiments of the game, only a tiny percentage of people are aware of its more difficult aspects; the vast majority of adults feeling that it is a mere 'parlour game' which is somehow 'beneath them'.

In fact, the 'fear' that the game is insufficiently difficult – an incredible notion for those in the know – can quickly be dispelled by playing a good player. In the past, because genuinely good players are rare, this was no easy task. Fortunately, in our modern computer age, this problem no longer exists. Chinook (a *very* good player!) is available to challenge on the following World Wide Web Site: http://www.cs.ualberta.ca/~chinook. Play it now!

In passing, it's also worth noting that:

1) No human being has come close to mastering the game.

2) To date, contrary to popular belief, no computer program has come close to mastering the game.

3) In a recent book, *Man v Machine: Kasparov-IBM's Deep Blue*, by Raymond Keene, Byron Jacobs and Tony Buzan, a draughts player, Dr Marion Tinsley, is put forward as one of the greatest, if not the greatest, mind sports champions of all time.

Appeal

Of course, merely being difficult does not qualify a game as a great game. The appeal of draughts is much deeper than that, and is best explained by quoting some of its followers:

'The public perception of checkers is that it is a game for children and old men. This is unfortunate; the game deserves to be more popular than it is... [It] has a beauty all its own, requiring a more delicate touch than does chess and a subtlety of play that rivals go. Unfortunately, the simplicity of the rules is often misconstrued. In fact, it is this simplicity that enhances the elegance of the game.' (Dr Jonathan

Schaeffer)

'Playing chess is like looking out over a limitless ocean; playing checkers is like looking into a bottomless well.' (Dr Marion Tinsley)

'A good game of checkers is like a great building – every brick fits right into place and, when the architect has drawn his plans correctly, the finished product is something to admire and enjoy.' (Richard Fortman)

'[Checkers is] an intellectual art in which knowledge, experience and individual ingenuity are essential to advancement; but of these requisites ingenuity (the inventive touch) is by far the most important.' (Willie Ryan)

'[Draughts is] a storehouse of wondrous things.' (Derek Oldbury)

'Checkers is a battle, and the ideas of the contestants are the weapons used.' (Edwin Hunt)

'Checkers as the experts play it, with all its richness of ideas and exquisite economy of force, is much more fun [than the casual version].' (Fred Reinfeld)

'[Draughts] is an art, the practice of which will enrich your life.' (Irving Chernev).

Draughts and Chess

Draughts has often suffered from comparison with chess. The truth is that the games are completely different: in their objectives, in their characters – English draughts represents the ultimate in minimalism – and in their rules. In particular, the fact that in draughts, since men cannot move backwards, every time you move one you are committing yourself: something which is central to the game's difficulty. They aren't even played on the same board! For instance, the Lallement board and the Roundsquare board – 'In every respect superior to the board generally in use' (Richard Jordan) – invented by William Call, remove the 32 non-playing squares and, because of the closer proximity of the pieces, make it easier to visualise and play blindfolded (without sight of the board).

Nonetheless, many chess players, from experts to World Champions, have taken an interest, to a greater or lesser extent, in draughts over the years, including Joseph Blackburne, Irving Chernev, Fred Reinfeld, Gerald Abrahams, Edward Lasker, Emanuel Lasker, Harry Pillsbury (a draughts master), Capablanca, Norman Littlewood, Tom Landry, George Miller, Rawle Allicock and, according to Frank Brady in his *Profile of a Prodigy*, Bobby Fischer.

'To me it is as silly to belittle chess as it is to downgrade checkers. For the most part, I have had but little difficulty in beating at either game those would-be chess players who belittle checkers and checker players. Checker players need not adopt a similar attitude.' (Dr Harry Langman)

Methodology

This book attempts to take the useful ideas and suggestions scattered hither and thither among the game's literature, and combine them with my own into an instructive and entertaining form. The role of strategy is emphasised throughout, and the key elements of space, time and force, first described explicitly by Derek Oldbury in *Move Over*, are presented afresh, together with numerous illustrative examples. After a couple of essential introductory chapters, the mastery of which will place you head and shoulders above the everyday player, the material is given with the endgame first through to the opening last. Though paradoxical, this is perfectly logical, and has been proven to be the most efficient way of gaining understanding. For consistency, all the chapters look at things from White's viewpoint; naturally the same ideas apply to the black forces. Every attempt has been made to give players credit where due, but most of the examples are so fundamental that this has generally not been appropriate. Suffice to say they are not original with me! Lastly, my thanks to Jim Loy for the use of his excellent diagram fonts.

 NOTE: Purely as a matter of convention, male pronouns are used throughout this book.

Chapter Two

Preliminaries

- Notation
- The Rules (in brief)

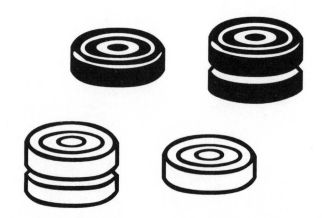

Notation

Before commencing study, you need to become familiar with the simple system used for recording the moves:

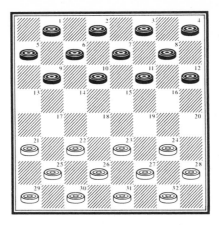

Diagram 1
The starting position

As can be seen, at the start of each game the black men are placed on squares 1 to 12, and the white men on squares 21 to 32. In accordance with normal procedure, throughout this book the white pieces will be shown moving up the board.

NOTE: In actual play the black squares are used, but in all publications the white squares are employed for clarity.

A move is recorded by means of two numbers separated by a hyphen. The numbers signify the squares on which a particular piece starts and finishes. A semi-colon is given after each white move.

NOTE: On rare occasions three numbers are required to record a move. I've only seen this four times in 21 years of tournament play!

As an aid to learning the numbers, you may initially find it helpful to:

- Purchase a numbered board; or
- Number the black squares with a Chinagraph pencil; or
- Use Diagram 1 as a guide.

Whichever approach is adopted, usage of the numbers will soon become automatic, and have the effect of making the board seem more compact and manageable. It will also allow you to delve into the game's substantial literature, skilfully chronicled in William Call's *The Literature Of Checkers* and Ken Lovell's *Draughts Books Of The Twentieth Century*.

Annotation Symbols

... White move follows

! indicates an excellent, possibly winning move.

? indicates a poor, possibly losing move.

!? indicates an interesting move.

?! indicates a dubious move.

Chess and draughts are often referred to as 'sister games', but they actually differ in a large number of ways. One of these is that in draughts it is Black, not White, who moves first. Remembering this, play through the following short game.

10-15 23-18; 12-16 21-17; 9-13 24-20; 16-19 17-14; 6-9 27-24; 1-6 32-27; 8-12 25-21; 12-16 27-23; 6-10? (A) 21-17! (B); 4-8 29-25; 8-12 25-21; 3-8 30-25; 2-6 31-27 (C). White wins.

A: Clearly Black was not even looking one move ahead when he played this loser. Better to look one move ahead in the right direction than twenty moves ahead in the wrong direction!

B: White sees that after 21-17 both sides will have four moves in hand, and that a complete block in his favour is inevitable.

C: Wrongly thought by the uninitiated to be a draw, this is actually a win for White, since he made the last move. The fact that all 24 men are still on the board, though unusual, is irrelevant.

The Rules (in brief)

I think you would be hard pressed to find a person over the age of ten who had not played at least one game of draughts in his life. However, though fairly familiar with the basic mechanics of play, namely **'move on the black squares and jump when you can!',** only a tiny percentage of people know the correct rules. Appendix 1, taken from *The EDA Handbook* (2nd Edition), gives these in detail, but for the moment the following will suffice:

1) The board is arranged, like chess, with a black square in the bottom left-hand corner (in official competitions a green and buff board is used).

2) Black always moves first. (In official competitions red and white pieces are used because, in combination with the green and buff board, they are easier on the eye, but the players are always referred to as 'Black' and 'White' regardless.)

3) Men can jump kings.

4) All jumps must be taken!

WARNING: This rule means what it says! There are no ifs, buts or ands.

5) If a player has a choice of jumps, he may select any one he wishes; not necessarily that which gains the most pieces.

6) A player wins either by removing all his opponent's pieces from the board or by rendering them immobile.

NOTE: 'Last move wins!'

7) When a man reaches the final row of the board (king-row) it becomes a king, and the player's move terminates. Kings can move both forwards and backwards.

NOTE: It follows that a man cannot jump into and out of the king-row in a single move.

Chapter Three

The Basics

- 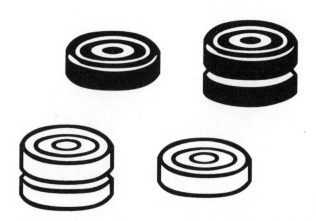 Elementary King Endings
- Elementary Tactics
- Try it Yourself

Elementary King Endings

In *The Murders in the Rue Morgue,* Edgar Allen Poe eloquently describes the subtlety and profundity of draughts. Unfortunately, much as I agree with his sentiments, it is evident from a later, neglected passage, that his actual understanding of the game was minimal. Namely, he describes a situation of two kings a side, and suggests this can be won by the player possessing the 'superior *acumen*'.

In fact, in a free and open position, 2 kings v 2 kings, 3 kings v 3 kings, 4 kings v 4 kings etc. is a dead draw; there being absolutely nothing to play for. One king against one requires special consideration, however, and is dealt with shortly.

Contrariwise, in a free and open position, 2 kings v 1 king, 3 kings v 2 kings, 4 kings v 3 kings etc. is a certain win for the side with the king majority. However, the winning techniques need to be learnt, and will be addressed.

Getting to know the Board

1) The long diagonal stretching from square 29 to square 4 (the two single-corner squares) is known as the 'single-corner diagonal'. This was christened the 'D[defensive]-line' by Derek Oldbury.

2) More generally, squares 4, 8, 11 and 12 are known as 'Black's single-corner', while squares 21, 22 ,25 and 29 are known as 'White's single-corner'.

3) The two diagonals stretching from square 32 to square 5, and square 1 to square 28 respectively, are known as the 'double-corner diagonals'. (Squares 28 and 32 being one double-corner, and squares 1 and 5 the other.) Oldbury called these the 'A[attacking]-lines'.

4) More generally, squares 1, 5, 6 and 9 are known as 'Black's double-corner', while squares 24, 27, 28 and 32 are known as 'White's double-corner'.

5) The two diagonals stretching from square 30 to square 12, and square 3 to square 21 respectively, are known, again courtesy of Oldbury, as the 'E[equality]-lines'.

6) In an endgame situation, a player is said to have 'the opposition' if he is in a position to *check the advance of opposing pieces beyond a certain point.* This concept will be expanded in the endgame section.

1 King v 1 King

Diagram 1
White to move and win

Diagram 2
White to move, Black draws

In Diagram 1, White has the opposition, and wins by pinning Black against the side of the board.

 TIP: Play through this several times, testing out all of Black's options.

One possible continuation would be ... 4-8; 29-25 8-11; 25-22 11-15; 22-17 15-18; 17-21 18-22 and White wins.

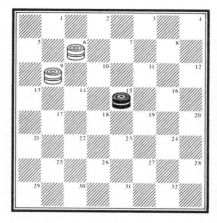

Diagram 3
White to move and win

Diagram 4
White to move and draw

In Diagram 2 White again has the opposition, but on this occasion Black has access to the double-corner diagonals, and hence the double-corner itself, and a see-saw draw results. Again, you should play this out.

Black draws after ... 5-9; 12-16 9-14; 16-19 14-18; 19-24! 18-23; 24-28 23-27; 28-32 etc.

2 Kings v 1 King

Winning with two kings against one from an open position is simplicity itself once the correct procedure is known. It falls into three phases:

1) The two kings force the lone king back into the double-corner (to retreat elsewhere would lead to instant defeat).

2) One of the two kings enters the double-corner, forcing the lone king out.

3) The lone king is pinned on the side of the board.

From Diagram 3 White wins with ... 9-14; 15-19 6-10; 19-23 10-15; 23-27 14-18; 27-24 18-23; 24-28 (phase 1) 15-19; 28-32 19-24; 32-28 23-19; 28-32 24-28 (phase 2); 32-27 28-32; 27-31 19-15! (19-23 allows 31-27 and wastes time); 31-26 15-18; 26-31 18-22.

William Payne, a mathematician, wrote the first draughts book in English, *An Introduction to the Game of Draughts*, in 1756. The position in Diagram 4, which further demonstrates the inherent restrictiveness of the single-corner zone, was featured, and shows that 1 king against 2 kings is not always a hopeless cause.

White draws as follows: ... 18-22; 30-25 22-26; 25-30 26-22 etc. (drawn by a see-saw operation).

3 Kings v 2 Kings

Here there are 3 cases to be considered:

1) Where the defending kings occupy opposite double-corners;

2) Where the defending kings occupy the same double-corner;

3) Where the defending kings occupy the same single-corner.

Diagram 5, though easy to win when you know how, is a frequent source of trouble for beginners. Indeed, many laymen are under the impression that no win can be forced. In fact, it is swiftly effected by constantly threatening, and eventually forcing, a simple exchange (one for one); reducing the situation to 2 kings against 1 and the win shown previously. The defender, of course, tries to avoid this.

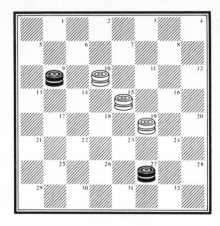

Diagram 5
White to move and win

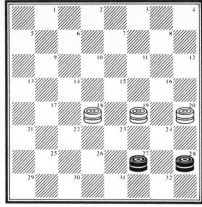

Diagram 6
White to move and win

In the above example White wins as follows: ... 15-18; 9-5 (9-13 loses quickly by 10-14) 10-6; 27-32 (if 5-1, White replies with 18-15) 19-23 (threatening 6-9); 5-1 (Black must move out of the way) 6-9; 32-28 (if 1-5, White replies with 9-14 creating the threat of two simple exchanges on his next move) 23-27 (forming the key position); 1-5 (28-32 amounts to the same thing) 27-23; 5-14 18-9 and White wins.

 TIP: In the endgame, particularly when defending, it is good policy, where possible, to keep your kings together. For one thing, no tactical opportunities are available otherwise.

Diagram 7
White to move and win

In Diagram 6, Black has succeeded in this goal, but White still wins by forcing a simple exchange. This is achieved with ... 19-23 (deemed a time-waster in many texts, but actually the best approach!); 28-32

(27-31 allows White to exchange immediately with 23-27) 20-16!; 27-31 (if 27-24, White replies with 18-15; and after 24-27 exchanges with 16-11, and after 24-20 exchanges with 23-18) 16-11!; 32-28 (if 31-27, White replies with 18-15) 11-15; 28-32 23-26; 31-22 18-25 etc.

In Diagram 7 White employs a neat sacrifice before clinching matters with a simple exchange. The solution is as follows: ... 15-10; 21-25 14-17; 22-26 17-21; 25-22 10-14; 26-23 14-17; 23-26 (22-18 allows White to win with either 17-14 or 17-22) 21-25! (just when White seemed to have achieved nothing); 22-29 17-22; 26-17 13-22. White wins.

NOTE: It is possible for 2 kings to draw against 3 using an extension of Diagram 4. Black kings on 21, 29 and 30; white kings on 18 and 23. White, to move, draws with ... 18-22; 30-25 23-18; 25-30 18-23 etc. (drawn by a see-saw operation).

Diagrams 8 through 11, though less general, illustrate other snappy ways of finishing off your opponent with 3 kings against 2, and are worthy of study.

 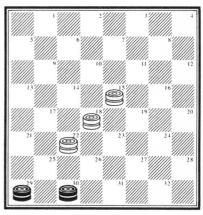

Diagram 8
White to move and win

Diagram 9
White to move and win

White wins in the following way: ... 18-14! (don't hesitate to give up 2 for 1 if it enables you to score a quick win); 25-9 5-14; 29-25 14-18.

In Diagram 9 White exploits his majority with ...15-11!; 30-25 18-15; 25-18 15-22.

In Diagram 10 White plays ... 16-19! (allowing Black a 2 for 1); 27-31 (if 27-24 20-27; 32-16 28-24 and White wins with the opposition) 20-24!; 32-27 (if 31-26, White exchanges with 19-23) 28-32! (not 24-20?, after which Black draws with 27-24); 27-20 19-24; 20-27 32-23 and White wins.

In Diagram 11 White wins after ... 23-26; 28-32 27-24!; 20-27 26-31 (the king is trapped).

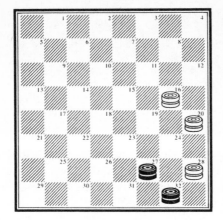

Diagram 10
White to move and win

Diagram 11
White to move and win

4 Kings v 3 Kings

Here there are 2 cases to consider:

1) Where there are 2 defending kings in one double-corner and 1 in the other;

2) Where the 3 defending kings are combined.

In the first case, the winning procedure is as follows:

a) Completely immobilise the unaccompanied defending king;

b) Line up the 4 kings to exchange off the lone king, reducing the situation to 3 kings against 2.

Diagram 12
White to move and win

Diagram 13
White to move and win

In Diagram 12 White wins in the following fashion: ... 18-15; 1-5 (White was threatening 9-6) 9-6; 28-32 15-10; 32-28 (5-1 allows 10-15) 6-1; 28-32 (if 5-9, White can reduce the forces with 19-23!; 27-18 10-14! – a device known as the breeches) 10-14 (the king is now immobilised); 32-28 20-16; 27-24 19-15; 24-27 16-11; 27-23 15-10; 28-24 11-7; 23-27 14-9; 5-14 10-17.

In Diagram 13, White forces Black back against the wall to reduce his mobility, then once more utilises a temporary sacrifice to win. This is achieved after ... 21-17! (the king on 22 has an important role to play); 27-31 (28-32 19-24; 27-31 24-28 just hastens the process) 20-24; 28-32 24-28; 31-27 19-16; 27-31 16-20; 31-27 22-26! (the killer); 30-23 28-24!; 27-31 24-27!; 31-24 20-18 and White wins.

 NOTE: It is possible, though highly unusual, for 3 kings to draw against 4. Black kings on 20, 28, 31 and 32; white kings on 18, 19 and 22. White, to move, draws with ... 18-23; 20-24 19-15; 31-27 22-18; 24-20 15-19; etc.

The procedure for winning with 5 kings to 4, 6 kings to 5 etc. is to:

Force your opponent's kings to the edges of the board where they have least mobility;

Exchange them off to reduce the situation to an ever-simpler state.

 TIP: Even in a clearly winning position, every effort should be taken to minimise your opponent's counterplay. That is, limit him to as few kings as possible. As Charles Barker once put it: 'If my opponent refuses to resign in a hopeless position, I end his discomfiture in the quickest manner possible.'

Elementary Tactics

The game of draughts consists of a subtle blend of strategy and tactics. Strategy involves long-term planning, while tactics are the various devices used to carry through a particular plan.

This chapter provides a comprehensive, step-by-step, guide to the elementary tactical devices (often termed the 'tricks of the trade').

As mentioned earlier, there are three elements operating in a game of draughts: space, time and force. Tactics operate in the element of force, and can bring about some very short games. For example:

9-13 22-18; 5-9? 18-15!; 11-18 (or 10-19) 23-5. White wins.

10-15 21-17; 12-16? 24-19!; 15-24 28-12. White wins.

Of course, in neither case is the game actually over but, with an expert handling the white pieces, the result is a foregone conclusion. The winning policy is to make a series of judicious (non position-weakening) exchanges until the situation is reduced to one of those dealt with earlier in the chapter. Needless to say, there is nothing discreditable in this; the twin objectives of the game being to obtain a winning position and then to win as efficiently as possible.

NOTE: In a free and open position, the gain of a single piece is enough to ensure a won game; the loss of a piece will lose the game.

Between novices, tactics naturally dominate: the result of the game often hinging on who makes the last blunder. Between experts, however, tactics become subservient to strategy and are used, by a combination of direct ('do something about this or else...') and indirect ('you can't go there because...') threats, to steer the opponent in a desired direction, rather than, except in a minority of cases, with the expectation of executing a coup. Hence, in the vast majority of top-class games, unless a man has been sacrificed on positional grounds, both sides will be equal in numbers until very near the end. Irving Chernev, author of the attractive and entertaining *The Compleat Draughts Player*, surprisingly stated that 'draughts is almost all tactics'. I would beg to differ.

NOTE: A thorough grounding in tactics is necessary, but not sufficient, if one wishes to become a master or grandmaster.

Elementary Tactical Devices

Of the many elementary tactical devices, nine deserve special consideration. We shall study these in turn.

NOTE: These devices are useful both for winning and for extricating a player from an apparently losing position.

In most cases the ideas have been presented in their starkest form, removing additional pieces which might be present in a game, in order to focus on the key points. Incidentally, any experts out there should solve all 114 examples and exercises inside 10 minutes, *without moving the pieces!*

TIP: Rather than memorise specific positions, you should seek to identify and learn the winning patterns or configurations. You should also try to invent your own examples. This is a valuable exercise that will speed your development.

1) 2 for 1

As the name implies, one piece is given up and two gained in return.

In Diagram 14 White wins with ...24-19; 15-24 28-12.

In Diagram 15 White wins with the sequence ... 25-22; 17-26 (or 18-25) 30-14.

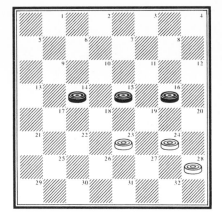

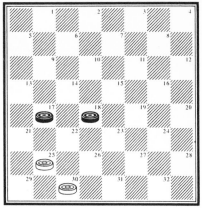

Diagram 14
White to move and win

Diagram 15
White to move and win

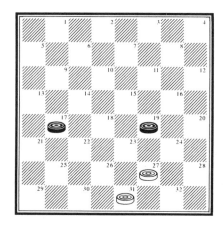

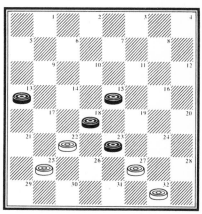

Diagram 16
White to move and win

Diagram 17
White to move and win

Diagram 16 is another straightforward example. White gains two for one with ... 27-23; 19-26 31-13.

In Diagram 17 White wins a piece after ... 25-21; 18-25 27-11.

2) 2 for 2

Two pieces are given up, two are gained in return and, in the examples selected, the game is won on position.

In Diagram 18 White wins with the sequence ... 20-16; 12-19 27-23; 19-26 31-13.

In Diagram 19 White exchanges two for two with ... 21-17; 14-21 28-24; 20-27 32-14.

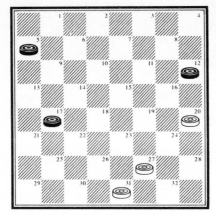

Diagram 18
White to move and win

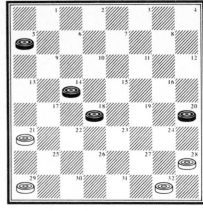

Diagram 19
White to move and win

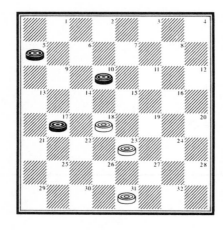

Diagram 20
White to move and win

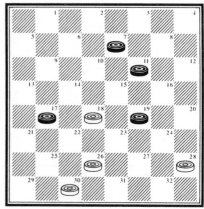

Diagram 21
White to move and win

In Diagram 20 White has the trick ... 18-15!; 10-26 31-13 and White wins.

In Diagram 21 White wins after the sequence ... 26-22!; 17-26 30-16; 11-20 18-15.

In Diagram 22 we see one further example. In this case White wins by first giving up two men: ... 11-8!; 4-11 18-15; 11-18 14-32 and White wins.

Diagram 22
White to move and win

3) 3 for 2

This is merely an extension of the 2 for 1; two pieces being given up and three gained in return.

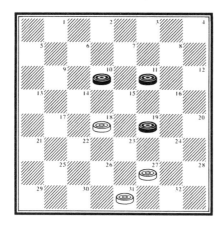 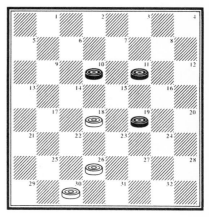

Diagram 23
White to move and win

Diagram 24
White to move and win

Firstly (Diagram 23), a simple of example of a 3 for 2. White wins after ... 18-15!; 11-18 27-23; 18-27 (or 19-26) 31-6.

Similarly in Diagram 24, White wins here with the sequence ... 18-14; 10-17 26-22; 17-26 30-7.

In Diagram 25 White wins after sacrificing two men with ... 19-15!; 10-19 (or 11-18) 26-22; 17-26 30-7.

In Diagram 26 White wins after ... 18-15!; 11-18 27-24; 20-27 32-5.

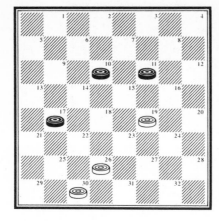

Diagram 25
White to move and win

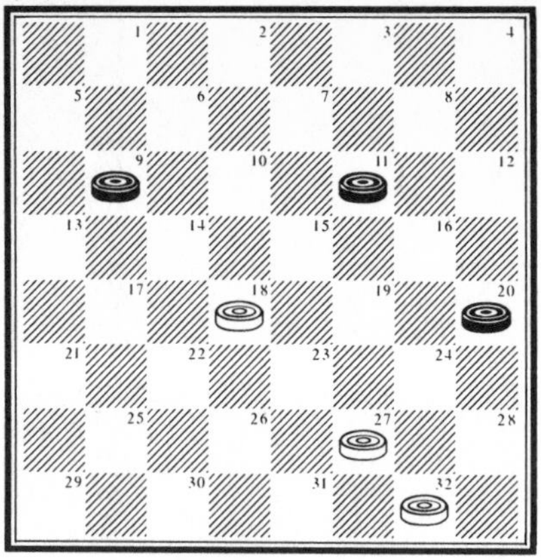

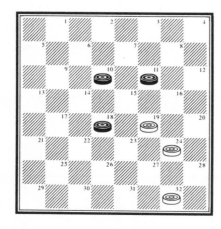

Diagram 27
White to move and win

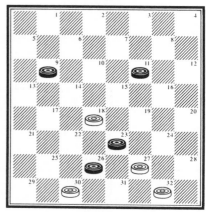

Diagram 26
White to move and win

Diagram 28
White to move and win

Diagram 27 is another reasonably straightforward example. White wins after ... 19-16; 11-27 32-7.

Diagram 28 is more tricky. White wins after ... 18-15!; 11-18 32-28; 23-32 30-5 and the two will defeat one.

In Diagram 29 White makes three jumps along the long diagonal after ... 20-16!; 11-20 22-17; 13-22 25-4 and White wins.

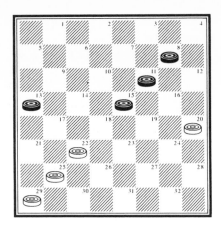

Diagram 29
White to move and win

4) Rebound

This is a double-action device, where one of the opponent's pieces is used as a backstop.

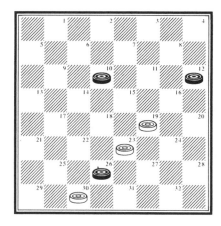

Diagram 30
White to move and win

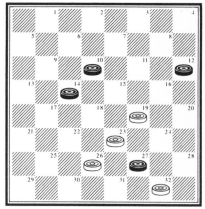

Diagram 31
White to move and win

In this first example of rebound (Diagram 30) White wins after ... 19-15; 10-19 23-16; 12-19 30-16.

Similarly in Diagram 31, White wins with ... 19-15; 10-19 23-16; 12-19 32-16.

Diagram 32 is a slightly more advanced example of the rebound theme. White wins after ... 28-24!; 20-27 26-22; 25-18 23-14; 9-18 32-14.

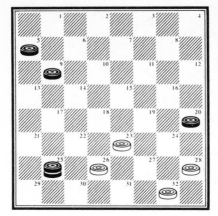

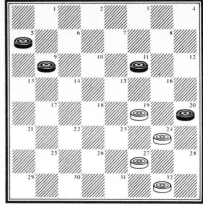

Diagram 32
White to move and win

Diagram 33
White to move and win

In Diagram 33 the winning sequence is ... 27-23; 20-27 19-15; 11-18 23-14; 9-18 32-14.

5) In-and-Out

This idea makes use of the fact that a player's move terminates when one of his men jumps (or moves) into the king-row, granting the opponent a 'free' move to set things up for a coup.

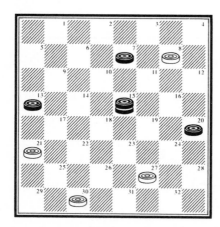

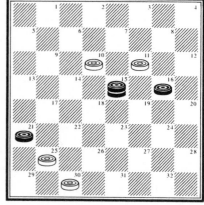

Diagram 34
White to move and win

Diagram 35:
White to move and win

For example, from Diagram 34 White wins after ... 21-17; 13-22 30-26; 22-31 8-3; 31-24 3-28.

In Diagram 35 White wins in a similar fashion with ... 10-7!; 15-8 30-26; 21-30 7-3; 30-23 3-26.

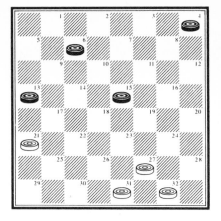 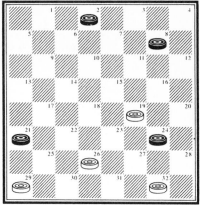

Diagram 36
White to move and win

Diagram 37
White to move and win

Once again (Diagram 36) White wins by allowing Black to promote with ... 21-17; 13-22 31-26; 22-31 32-28; 31-24 28-1.

In Diagram 37 the solution is ... 29-25!; 21-30 32-28; 30-16 28-3.

 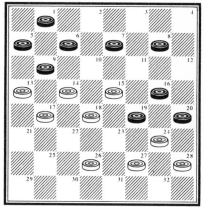

Diagram 38
White to move and win

Diagram 39
White to move and win

Diagram 38 is a more difficult version of the in and out theme. White wins after ... 27-24! (getting into position); 20-27 (you should work out how 28-19 loses in a similar fashion) 23-32; 28-24 29-25; 21-30 32-28; 30-23 28-26.

Diagram 39 is another more complicated example. White wins in the following fashion: ... 15-10! (giving up 3 men is fine if it wins); 6-31 13-6; 1-10 24-6; 31-24 28-3.

6) Double-Corner Devices

A collection of coups based around common configurations of pieces in the double-corner zone.

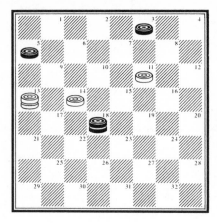

Diagram 40
White to move and win

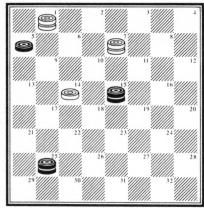

Diagram 41
White to move and win

In Diagram 40 White wins in the following fashion: ... 11-7; 3-17 (18-9 also loses) 13-15.

In Diagram 41 White allows two jumps and wins after ... 14-9!; 5-14 7-10!; 15-6 1-17 and White has the opposition.

Diagram 42
White to move and win

Diagram 43
White to move and win

In Diagram 42 the solution is ... 13-9; 5-14 7-10; 15-6 2-18 and once again White wins due to having the opposition.

On this occasion (Diagram 43) White wins despite having no kings to

Black's two. The winning sequence is ... 14-10; 5-14 6-2!; 15-6 2-18 and White has the opposition.

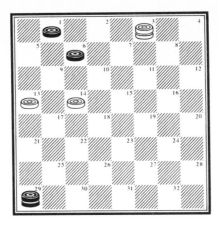

Diagram 44
White to move and win

Here's a slightly more complex version of the theme. White wins after ... 3-7 (threatening 7-2, winning the man on 6); 6-10 13-9; 10-17 9-6; 1-10 7-21.

7) Breeches

The situation where a king is placed between two opposing pieces, gaining one of them on the next move. There are also double breeches and triple breeches; the latter being extremely rare.

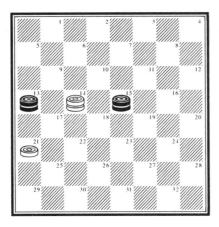

Diagram 45	**Diagram 46**
White to move and draw	White to move and win

Diagram 45 is the most basic example. White draws with ... 21-17; 13-

22 14-18.

Diagram 46 is another simple example. Here White wins with ... 16-12; 8-11 12-16; 11-15 16-19.

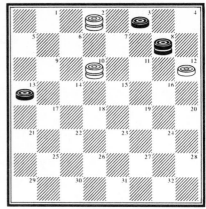

Diagram 47
White to move and draw

Diagram 48
White to move and win

White looks to be in trouble in Diagram 47, but can draw in the following way: ... 3-8; 11-15 19-16; 12-19 8-11; 15-18 11-15.

In Diagram 48 White wins with the sequence ... 2-7!; 13-17 10-14!; 3-10 12-3.

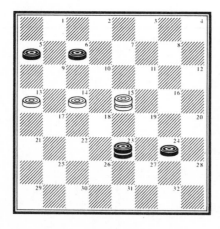

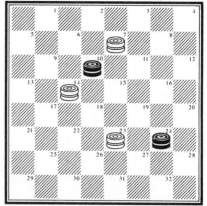

Diagram 49
White to move and draw

Diagram 50
White to move and win

In Diagram 49 White is a man down, but can draw after ... 14-9; 5-14 15-18. This is known as the double breeches for obvious reasons.

White is losing a king in Diagram 50, but can still win after ... 23-19; 24-15 14-18; (7-11 also wins) 15-22 (10-3 also loses) 7-14.

Diagram 51
White to move and win

In Diagram 51 White is again losing a king, but can still win after ...
19-23!; 27-9 7-5.

8) Fork

When a king attacks a man from behind, it is known as a press. A fork
is when a king presses two men simultaneously, gaining one of them
on the next move.

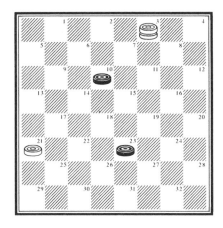

Diagram 52
White to move and win

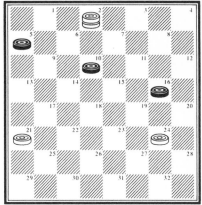

Diagram 53
White to move and win

In Diagram 52 the white king presses the black man to set up an
eventual fork. White wins after ... 3-7 (press); 10-15 7-10 (press); 15-
19 10-15 (press); 19-24 15-19.

White wins in the following way in Diagram 53: ... 24-20 (forcing the man on 16 into harm's way: a press from the front, like this, is known as a squeeze); 16-19 2-7; 10-14 7-10; 14-18 10-15.

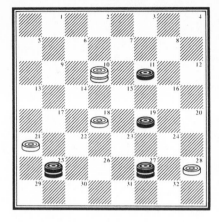

Diagram 54
White to move and win

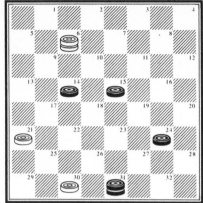

Diagram 55
White to move and draw

From Diagram 54 White wins in the following way: ... 18-15; 11-18 10-15. As you might expect, this is known as a double fork.

White draws in Diagram 55 after ... 30-26! (not 6-10?, which loses by 15-18 and 18-22); 31-22 6-10. Drawn. Blundering into this position cost Willie Ryan a win in the 1937 US National Tournament.

9) Optional Jumps

Giving the opponent the choice of two or more jumps.

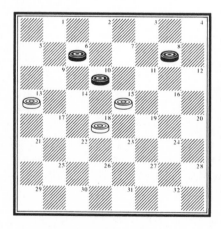

Diagram 56
White to move and draw

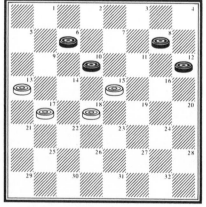

Diagram 57
White to move and draw

In Diagram 56 White's man on 15 is attacked, but White can draw by giving his opponent an option with ... 13-9; 6-13 (or 10-19) 15-6.

In Diagram 57 White draws with the sequence ... 17-14; 10-19 (or 10-17) 18-15; 19-23 14-9 (not 14-10? – can you see why?). Winning a man by the use of a squeeze, as here, is known as a steal.

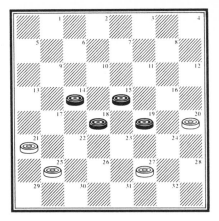

Diagram 58
White to move and draw

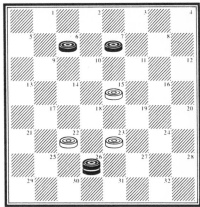

Diagram 59
White to move and draw

White looks to be in real danger in Diagram 58, but can draw after ... 20-16; 19-23 25-22; 23-32 (18-25 loses of course) 22-17.

In Diagram 59 White draws cleverly with ... 15-10!; 6-15 (or 7-14) 23-18; 26-17 18-2. Drawn.

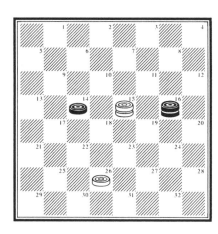

Diagram 60
White to move and win

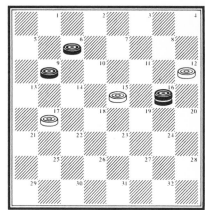

Diagram 61
White to move and draw

In Diagram 60 White wins after ... 26-22; 14-18 15-11!; 18-25 (or 16-7) 11-20; 25-30 20-24 and White has the opposition.

Despite having no king, White can draw in Diagram 61 with ... 12-8;

16-11 17-14!; 9-18 8-3; 11-16 15-11; 16-7 3-1.

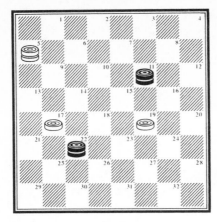

Diagram 62
White to move and win

Diagram 63
White to move and win

In Diagram 62 White wins after ... 19-15 (otherwise Black picks up the isolated man on 19, playing 22-26 and 26-23); 11-18 17-14; 18-9 5-14. White wins.

In Diagram 63, if White plays ... 1-5, Black gains the man on 25, playing 26-22. Instead White wins with ...21-17(this enables White to gain a tempo); 26-22 17-14; 22-29 1-5; 18-9 5-14.

Miscellaneous Examples

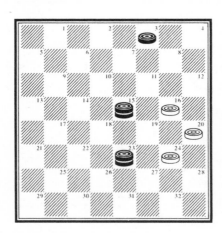

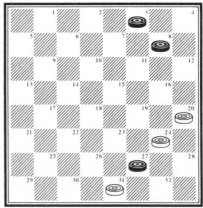

Diagram 64
White to move and win

Diagram 65
White to move and win

In Diagram 64 White wins with the sequence ... 16-11; 15-8 24-19; 23-16 20-4.

In Diagram 65 White wins with ... 24-19; 27-32 31-27; 32-16 20-4.

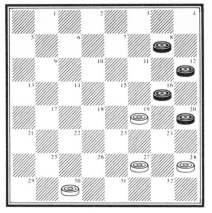

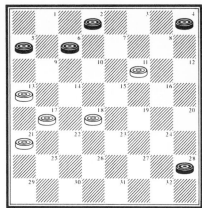

Diagram 66
White to move and win

Diagram 67
White to move and draw

Diagram 66: ... 19-15; 16-19 30-26; 12-16 15-11! (Black was intending to line up with 8-12); 8-15 26-22. White wins. In Tom Wiswell's words: 'Position beats possession.'

Diagram 67: ... 11-7! (vital: anything else leads to a slow death; Black taking a 2 for 1 with 6-9 at some point); 2-11 18-14 (the desired set-up); 28-32 14-9; 5-14 17-1. Drawn.

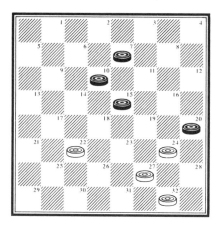

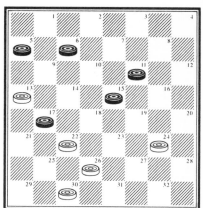

Diagram 68
White to move and win

Diagram 69
White to move and win

Willie Ryan termed the position in Diagram 68 a double exposure slip. White wins after ... 27-23!; 20-27 23-18; 7-11 32-23.

Note the similarity in Diagram 69 with the previous example. Here White wins after ... 26-23!; 17-26 23-19; 6-10 30-23. White wins.

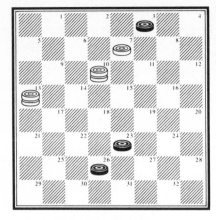

Diagram 70
White to move and win

Diagram 71
White to move and win

In Diagram 70 White wins after 10-14; 3-17 13-31. Arthur Reisman aptly entitled this the stretch.

Mr Reisman called the position in Diagram 71 the cross-country shot. White wins after ... 30-25!; 29-22 13-9; 22-13 6-1; 13-6 1-28.

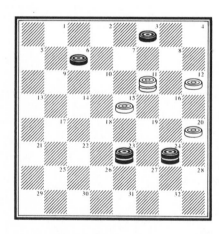

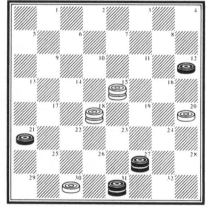

White to move and win
Diagram 72

Diagram 73
White to move and win

In Diagram 72 White wins in the following manner: ... 12-8!; 3-12 20-16!; 12-19 15-10; 6-15 11-20. This is commonly known as the whirligig shot, for reasons which should be apparent.

In Diagram 73 after ... 30-26; 31-22 18-25; 21-30 20-16; 12-19 15-31 White has the opposition and wins.

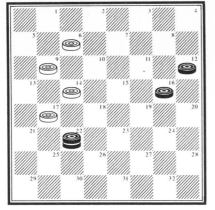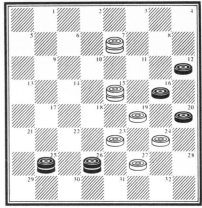

Diagram 74
White to move and win

Diagram 75
White to move and win

On this occasion (Diagram 74) Black is able to fork with his king, but it is to no avail. White wins after ... 17-13; 22-17 14-10; 17-14 (forking) 6-2!; 14-5 13-9!; 5-7 2-20.

In Diagram 75 White wins after ... 23-18!; 16-32 7-11; 20-27 11-16; 12-19 15-29. This is known as the swing around shot. It may surprise you to learn that this is a position of common occurrence. Indeed, had Black played 26-22, instead of 30-25?, which formed the position, he would have sustained a comfortable man-down draw: the three men on 12, 16 and 20 holding those on 19, 23, 24 and 27.

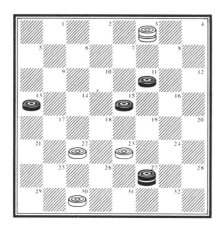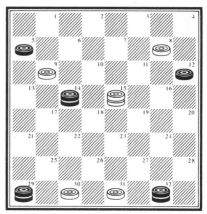

Diagram 76
White to move and win

Diagram 77
White to move and win

Entitled the spread eagle theme, Diagram 76 is a startling example of how one piece can beat two. White wins with ... 22-18!; 15-22 30-25!; 27-18 3-8; 22-29 8-22.

In Diagram 77 White wins after four sacrifices and a quadruple jump after ... 30-25! (or 31-27 first); 29-22 31-27!; 32-23 15-10!; 14-7 8-3; 5-14 3-19.

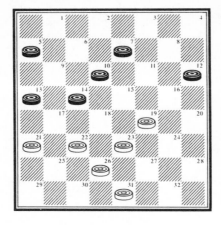

Diagram 78
White to move and win

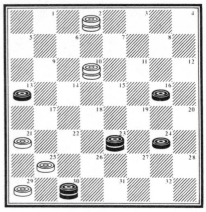

Diagram 79
White to move and win

In Diagram 78 White sets up a triple jump and wins after ... 19-15!; 10-19 23-16; 12-19 22-17; 13-22 26-3.

In Diagram 79 White wins after ... 21-17!; 13-22 (or 30-7) 25-18; 23-7 2-27. Derek Oldbury *almost* hooked Dr Marion Tinsley with this in their 3-Move World Championship Match of 1958.

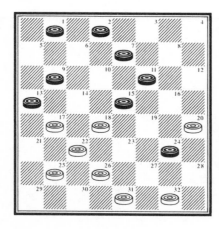

Diagram 80
White to move and win

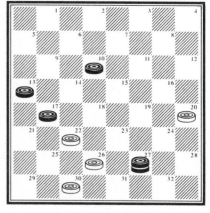

Diagram 81
White to move and win

In Diagram 80 White wins by an imaginative way of gaining a tempo: ... 18-14!; 9-18 25-21!; 18-25 32-28; 13-22 28-3. If you saw this, you are making exceptional progress!

Diagram 81 is an example of a very handy waiting move. White wins after ... 26-23; 17-26 20-16 (the waiting move); 27-18 30-7. White wins.

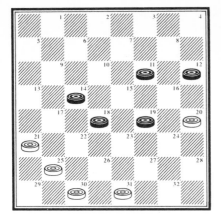

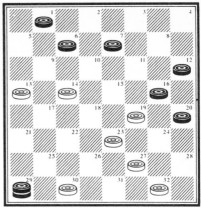

Diagram 82
White to move and win

Diagram 83
White to move and win

In Diagram 82 White wins after ... 21-17!; 14-21 30-26!; 21-30 26-23; 18-27 (or 19-26) 31-8; 30-26 8-3; 26-23 3-7; 23-19 7-10. This ending, known as First Position, is dealt with in depth in Chapter 4: Situations.

In Diagram 83 White wins after ... 23-18!; 16-23 30-25!; 29-15 27-2 (the man on 6 is trapped).

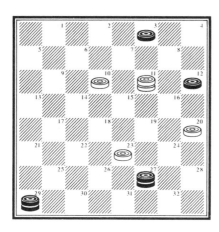

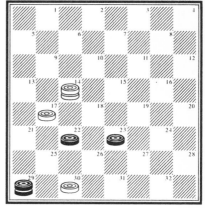

Diagram 84
White to move and win

Diagram 85
White to move and win

In Diagram 84 White wins with ... 10-7!; 27-18 20-16!; 3-10 (or 12-19) 11-7; 12-19 7-16; 29-25 16-19; 25-22 19-23. This beautiful idea is known as squaring the circle.

The winning sequence in Diagram 85 is ... 17-13; 22-26 (23-27 loses by 13-9; 27-31 14-17: Black lacks a waiting move) 14-17; 26-31 30-25; 29-22 17-19.

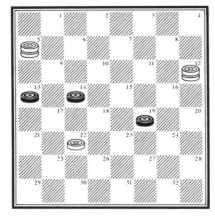

Diagram 86
White to move and win

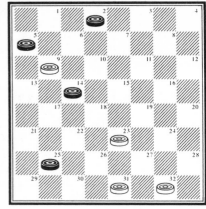

Diagram 87
White to move and draw

In Diagram 86 White makes good use of his two kings and wins by ... 5-9; 14-17 12-16; 17-26 16-30.

White's man on 9 looks to be in trouble in Diagram 87, but White can save the draw with ... 23-18!; 14-23 31-27; 5-14 27-9. Drawn.

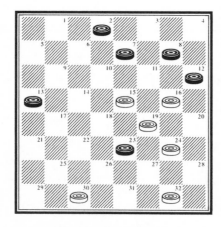

Diagram 88
White to move and win

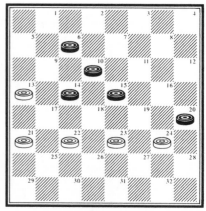

Diagram 89
White to move and win

The example in Diagram 88 is known as a pitch and squeeze play. White wins with ... 16-11! (Black was threatening a 2 for 1 with 7-11, but this turns the tables); 7-16 24-20. Black must lose 2 men.

In Diagram 89 White wins after ... 24-19; 15-24 22-18. With the man removed from 2, the 'elbow' formed by the men on 6, 10 and 14 is particularly vulnerable to attack.

Diagram 90
White to move and win

Diagram 91
White to move and draw

Diagram 90 is a very common way of relieving a single-corner 'cramp'. White wins after ... 22-18; 13-22 18-9; 5-14 25-9.

In Diagram 91 White must counter the obvious threat of 10-15. White can draw with... 32-28!; 10-15 20-16!; 12-19 27-24; 15-22 24-8.

Diagram 92
White to move and win

Diagram 93
White to move and win

Diagram 92 is more complex. White wins as follows: ... 23-18; 1-5 32-27; 5-9 (10-14 18-9; 5-14 27-23; 13-17 23-18; 14-23 21-14; loses by First Position) 27-23; 12-16 (10-14 loses by 18-15) 20-11; 10-15 21-17!; 15-22 (13-22 loses by 11-7) 23-18; 22-26 17-14.

In Diagram 93 White wins after ... 21-17!; 14-21 15-18; 24-15 18-11. Notice how the white king on 22 defeats two black men.

Diagram 94
White to move and win

Diagram 95
White to move and draw

In Diagram 94 Black's king is forking two white men, but White can use this to his advantage after ... 15-11; 19-12 9-6; 12-16 6-2; 16-7 2-11. White wins.

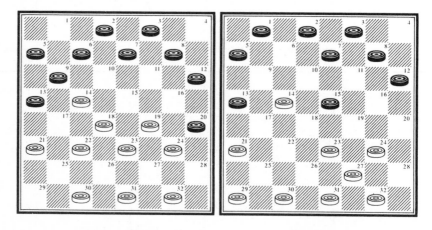

Diagram 96
White to move and win

Diagram 97
White to move and win

Despite the level material White's fighting for the draw in Diagram 95. This can be achieved in the following way: ... 10-14 (10-7 loses by 27-24); 27-23 19-15!; 11-18 13-9!; 23-26 14-30; 5-14 30-25!; 14-17 25-21; 17-22. Drawn.

In Diagram 96 White wins after ... 14-10!; 7-14 22-17!; 13-22 30-26; 20-27 26-1. The black man on 27 has been left 'hanging'.

In Diagram 97 White wins with ... 21-17!; 13-22 14-10!; 7-14 23-18; 14-23 27-4 (the man on 22 is doomed). Known as the blind shot, this has even caught experts out on occasion.

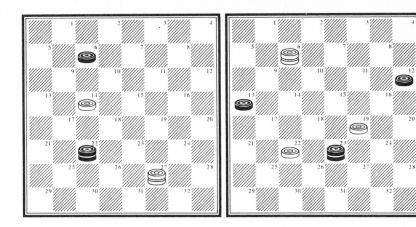

Diagram 98
White to move and draw

Diagram 99
White to move and draw

In Diagram 98 White is about to lose a man, but can still draw after ... 27-23; 22-17 14-9; 6-13 23-18; 17-21 18-22; 21-17 22-18.

Similarly in Diagram 99, White again loses a man, but salvages a draw with the sequence ... 6-10; 23-16 10-15; 16-20 15-19; 20-16 19-15.

Diagram 100
White to move and draw

Diagram 101
White to move and win

In Diagram 100 White can draw, despite being a man down, after ... 26-22; 21-25 22-18; 14-23 19-26; 25-30 26-22. (see Diagram 4)

On this occasion (Diagram 101) 1 king beats 2 men after ... 19-15; 10-19 26-23; 19-26 31-22.

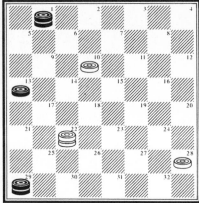

Diagram 102
White to move and draw

Diagram 103
White to move and win

In Diagram 102 White draws, despite having a man less, after ... 18-23; 10-15 22-25! (holds everything); 30-26 23-30; 15-18 25-22!; 18-25 30-26; 25-29 26-30; 29-25 30-26.

In this final example (Diagram 103) White wins with ... 28-24; 1-5 (Black must dislodge the king from 22) 24-19; 5-9 19-15; 9-14 22-26!; 14-7 26-22!; 7-2 15-10.

The last 6 examples show how it is possible to draw, or even win, with a piece short. This is discussed further in the endgame section.

Try it Yourself

 TIP: With the exercises, I would advise you to take no more than two minutes over each, referring to the solutions, without guilt, if stuck!

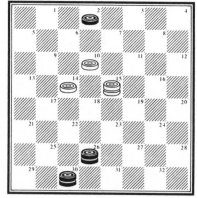

Exercise 1: 2 for 1
White to move and win

Exercise 2: 2 for 2
White to move and win

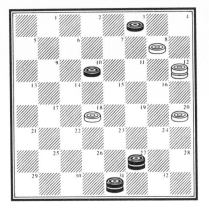

Exercise 3: 2 for 2
White to move and win

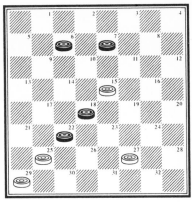

Exercise 4: 3 for 2
White to move and win

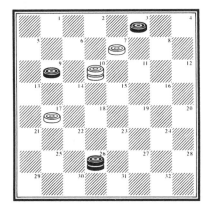

Exercise 5: 3 for 2
White to move and win

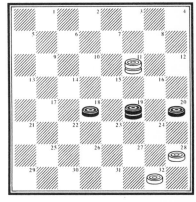

Exercise 6: 3 for 2
White to move and win

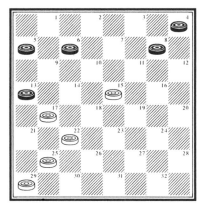

Exercise 7: Rebound
White to move and win

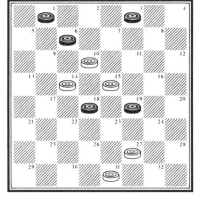

Exercise 8: Rebound
White to move and draw

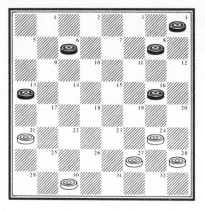

Exercise 9: In-and-Out
White to move and win

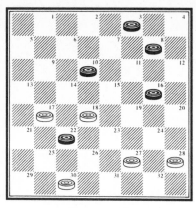

Exercise 10: In-and-Out
White to move and win

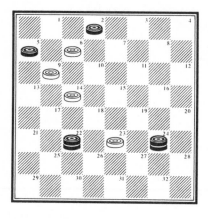

Exercise 11: D-C Devices
White to move and win

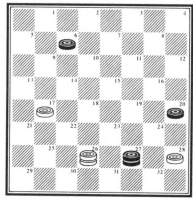

Exercise 12: Breeches
White to move and win

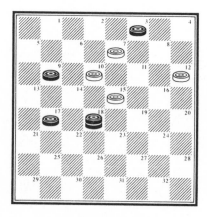

Exercise 13: Fork
White to move and draw

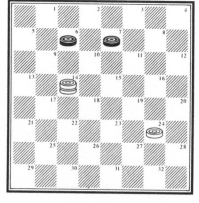

Exercise 14: Fork
White to move and win

Exercise 15: Optional Jumps
White to move and win

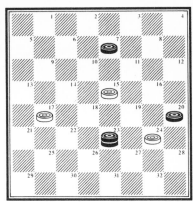

Exercise 16: Optional Jumps
White to move and draw

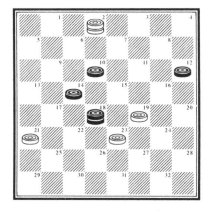

Exercise 17: Miscellaneous
White to move and win

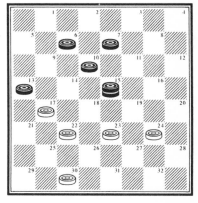

Exercise 18: Miscellaneous
White to move and win

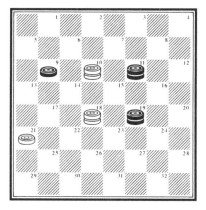

Exercise 19: Miscellaneous
White to move and win

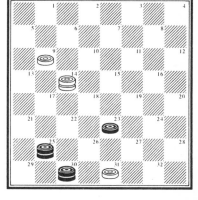

Exercise 20: Miscellaneous
White to move and win

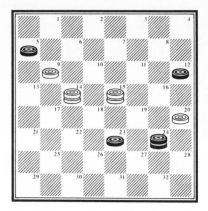

Exercise 21: Miscellaneous
White to move and win

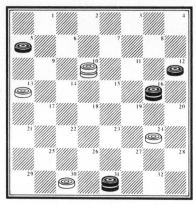

Exercise 22: Miscellaneous
White to move and win

Exercise 23: Miscellaneous
White to move and win

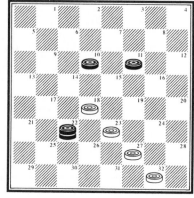

Exercise 24: Miscellaneous
White to move and win

Summary

- 1 king v 1 king is a win if you have the opposition and can prevent your opponent gaining access to the double-corner diagonals.

- In a free and open position, 2 kings defeat a lone king by forcing it to retreat to, and then ousting it out of, the double-corner.

- Other majority king endings are won by reducing the mobility of your opponent's kings and then forcing an exchange, or series of exchanges.

- Though unusual, it is possible to draw with a king short.

- It is not necessary, or helpful, to memorise the solutions to specific positions; it is the winning ideas which need to be learnt.

- If at any time during the game you gain a piece, and your opponent has no compensation, you should win.

- Many tactical devices exist, and a thorough knowledge of these is necessary, but not sufficient, in order to make headway.

- Identify the winning tactical patterns: don't attempt to memorise specific positions.

Chapter Four

The Endgame

- 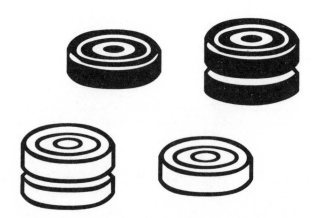 **Introduction**
- **Situations**
- **Themes**

Introduction

Definition: 'An endgame is a game ending, in which both sides have achieved a king; or at least have gained a clear run to the king-row.' (Derek Oldbury)

Because there are comparatively few pieces on the board, many players relax in the endgame, under the impression that there is 'nothing there'. This attitude should be guarded against at all costs.

 WARNING: 'In the endgame there are more squares to go wrong on.' (Tom Wiswell)

The relative importance of the endgame would appear to be a matter for some debate:

'One need only define the purpose of the endgame to see that this must be the most vital phase of the game... In draughts the best player wins, and the proof is here – in the endgame.' (Derek Oldbury)

'Most games are won, lost or drawn in the course of the midgame, and the more skilfully one manages it, the less important, as a rule, becomes the endgame play.' (Louis Ginsberg)

'The midgame is undoubtedly the meat in every game.' (Maurice Chamblee)

'If you master the opening and midgame, then there are no endgame difficulties.' (Basil Case)

While Ginsberg's argument carries a lot of weight – 75% of master games never reach an endgame – the caveat is that, in many cases, the players have anticipated and avoided difficulties. In other words, the endgames take place 'in the notes'.

Dozens of books have been devoted to the endgame, and are often very specialised. For example, *Midget Problems*, by William Call, considers only positions with two pieces per side! The 11 tips which follow are therefore, by necessity, of a very general nature.

 TIP 1: Identify the key features of the situation (This chapter – situations).

For example, Black, a piece down, observes that he is currently holding a white man on square 20, has the opposition, and can obtain two kings to oppose White's two kings. He will therefore angle for Payne's Single-Corner Draw.

 NOTE: Although the classic endgames tend to be diagrammed at a particular point, it is essential to realise that many thousands of positions are embraced by their defining features.

 TIP 2: Try and get ahead in development.

Assigning a score of 1 (move) for a man on the first row, 2 for one on the second row, 3 for one on the third row... up to 8 for a king, it is possible to determine which side is ahead in development, and by how many moves. In the late midgame and endgame *it is an advantage to be ahead in development*, and those exchanges which serve to boost your pull in this aspect of time should be sought. Achieving a particular goal or objective, *before your opponent*, may only be possible if you have this edge.

TIP 3: Position your kings judiciously.

Centralise them. From the centre, a king can get to any square on the board in just a few moves. This affords flexibility in both attack and defence.

Connect them. Whether attacking or defending, connected kings are far more formidable than separated kings.

Don't allow them to tread on each other's toes! When crowning several kings on a crowded board, it is very easy for your pieces to block each other's path, and cause a lot of wasted motion. In draughts, economy is always the watchword, so you need to plan to avoid this.

TIP 4: Be alert to the ways in which one king can hold two pieces.

In all of the following positions it is Black to move.

- Black men on 5 and 13; white king on 14. White wins.

- Black men on 13 and 21; white king on 22. White wins.

- Black man on 13, black king on 29; white king on 21 or 22. White wins.

- Black man on 5, black king on 13; white king on 14. Drawn.

- Black man on 13, black king on 21; white king on 22. Drawn.

- Black man on 21, black king on 29; white king on 13 or 22 or 23 or 30. Drawn.

- Black men on 4 and 12; white king on 11. Drawn.

- Black men on 12 and 20; white king on 19. Drawn.

- Black man on 4, black king on 12; white king on 11. Drawn.

- Black man on 12, black king on 20; white king on 19. Drawn.

- Black man on 28, black king on 32; white king on 23. White wins.

NOTE: These holds are useful both on their own and as part of a more complex board arrangement.

TIP 5: Recognise the winning potential afforded by a 'pivot man'.

Consider a kings and man, or men, endgame, in which the forces are *numerically equal*, and one of the opposing men is held, or can be held, immobile on a vertical edge of the board: known as the pivot man.

Assuming the defending king, or kings, to be on the same side of the board as the pivot man – no advantage can result otherwise – the general strategy is as follows:

1) Attack the defending king or kings. Render them immobile or threatened with immobility.

2) Thus force the man to move into a less favourable position.

3) Repeat the process, as required, until the man is virtually forced to assist the attacking kings, by 'getting in the way' of his fellow king, or kings. This will render it, or them, immobile.

WARNING: The attacked king or kings must not be allowed to escape to another area of the board. For example, from one double-corner zone to the other.

TIP 6: Recognise the drawing potential afforded by a pivot man

Consider an endgame in which the forces are *numerically unequal*, but in which the weaker force is able to hold one of the opponent's men immobile on a vertical edge of the board. If the defending kings can be forced to release the pivot man then the numerically superior side will win. If they cannot, then a draw will result. The usual method of driving off, or attempting to drive off, the defending kings is to attack one of the kings and, by rendering it immobile, force the other king, or kings, to relinquish the grip on the pivot man.

TIP 7: Be aware of the strengths and weaknesses of a bridge.

If White has retained men on 30 and 32 then, in order to crown, Black will either need to post a man on 21 and enter the restrictive single-corner via 22-25, or form a bridge by posting a man on 23, and pass under it with 22-26 or 24-27.

If Black can get in and out of the bridge, preferably with two or more kings, before White is in a position to attack then, with level pieces, he may have little to fear. Indeed, given the retarded development of the white men, he may hold the advantage.

If, however, Black is tied down to the defence of the man on 23 (which is a target for attack from four possible directions), as is often the case, and White can attack with his king(s), then, with level pieces, White may have good winning chances. In similar situations, White may utilise the weakness of the black man on 23 to obtain a draw a piece down. Another determining factor is the opposition.

NOTE: Bridge endgames are notoriously difficult to judge and, as a rule, rather than crown under a bridge, you would be well advised to break your opponent's king-row defence if the opportunity arises.

There are 2 main methods:

1) Black could line up three men on 14, 18 and 23 and exchange 23-27; or three men on 16, 19 and 23 and exchange 23-26.

2) Black could crown on 31; post a man on 15; give up the man on 23 by playing 23-26 or 23-27 as appropriate; regain the lost man by playing 31-26 or 31-27 as required.

A so-called 'secondary bridge' is formed when White retains men on 29 and 31, and Black, who posts a man on 22, crowns by passing under the bridge via 21-25 or 23-26. Such bridges do not have the characteristics or importance of the regular bridge,.

WARNING: None of the foregoing is meant to imply that White should make a general policy of retaining men on 30 and 32. In many cases this would be disastrous!

TIP 8: Improve your understanding of the endgame by learning the ideas embodied by the thirteen major endgame themes (This chapter – Themes).

TIP 9: Study problems, particularly the 'natural' kind, to increase the range of stratagems at your command and enhance your powers of visualisation.

TIP 10: Assess the status of the opposition.

Many 'academic' articles have been devoted to the thorny subject of the opposition – confusingly referred to by draughts players as 'the Move' – over the years; the vast majority serving only to cloud and muddle what is basically a straightforward concept.

'Of all the nonsense and over-emphasised banter which some writers have imposed on the principles of scientific play, no angle has been played up more often than this [opposition] business.' (Willie Ryan)

Definition: 'To have the opposition is to be in a position to *check the advance of opposing pieces beyond a certain point*.' (Derek Oldbury)

The opposition only comes into play in the endgame. It is not a relevant factor – essentially does not exist – in the opening and midgame.

NOTE: Many writers, including Gerald Abrahams, have confused the opposition with the relative state of development of the two sides. Both concepts operate in the element of time, but are otherwise completely different.

The opposition is only one factor among many in the endgame. Its relevance and relative importance depend upon the particular situation under consideration.

It is possible to have the opposition and lose! – a fact which many authors fail to note (for example, see Diagrams 33-35 in this chapter).

TIP 11: When it is your turn to move, to determine which side has the opposition simply pair-off the pieces; no counting is necessary.

Equal endgames

Diagram 1
White to move

Diagram 2
White to move

In Diagram 1 pair-off 12 and 19 (there is one intervening square). Mentally move ... 23-27; and you can see that White has the opposition, since 27 and 28 pair-off (there is one intervening square). Incidentally, when pairing-off in this way, you treat the rest of the board as if it were empty each time.

In Diagram 2 pair-off 21 and 30, and 20 and 27. Mentally move ... 32-28; 25-22 28-24; 22-18 24-19; and you can see that White again has the opposition.

Unequal endgames

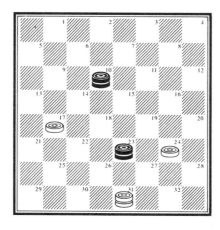

Diagram 3
Either to move: Black draws

For the purposes of pairing-off in these cases, ignore the pivot man, and consider only the active pieces.

In Diagram 3 Black is to move: 10-15 17-14; 23-19 (forcing the white man into 20, creating a pivot) 24-20; 15-11 (Black now holds the white man on 20 and has the opposition on the active white pieces: pair-off 11 and 14, and 19 and 31) 14-10; 19-15 10-6; 11-8 6-2; 15-11 etc. and the position is drawn (Payne's Single-Corner Draw – see Situations).

White to move: ... 24-20; 23-18 (holding the white man on 20 would not work, since White would have the opposition, so Black forces the other white man into 13, creating a pivot) 20-16; 18-14 17-13; 10-15 (pair-off 15 and 16, and 14 and 31, and you will see that Black has the opposition) 16-12; 15-11 31-27; 11-7 12-8; 7-2 8-3; 2-6 etc. and it's drawn (Roger's Draw – see Situations).

Changing the Opposition in an equal Endgame

There are two main methods:

a) By exchanging

The most common method of changing the opposition is by an exchange of pieces. However, there are many different types of exchange, and some alter the opposition, while others do not. Rather than attempt to memorise a lot of confusing and unnecessary 'rules' governing these exchanges, it is far wiser that you study each endgame in a normal fashion, with all the contingencies which this implies. In the course of your study, pair-off pieces as required to determine if the opposition has changed hands.

b) By entering the 'dog-hole'

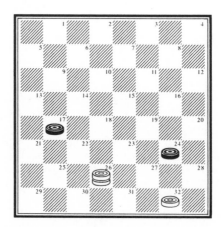

Diagram 4
White to move and win

Normally there has to be one intervening square for one piece to contain, or hold off, another. However, a man in the dog-hole (squares 5 and 28) can be contained by a piece on an adjoining square (squares 1 and 32), and this has implications for the opposition.

In this example Black has the opposition, but White effects a quick reversal with ... 26-31; 24-28 (forced) 31-26; 17-21 26-22. White has the opposition and wins!

Examples of the Opposition

These examples are of a fairly advanced nature. You may choose to try and solve them without looking at the solutions. Alternately, you may prefer to simply play through the solutions: equally instructive and less time-consuming.

NOTE: Diagrams 5-8 illustrate the most common way of changing the opposition.

Diagram 5
White to move and win.

Diagram 6
White to move and win.

A quick examination of Diagram 5 will reveal that Black currently possesses the opposition. White reverses this by forcing a simple exchange (a 1 for 1 where one of the capturing pieces is removed from the board). ... 2-7!; 9-13 7-11!; 26-31 (13-17 loses by the breeches) 18-23; 13-17 11-16!; 17-22 16-20!; 22-25 23-27 31-24 20-27. White wins.

In Diagram 6 White wins after ... 11-15; 17-22 15-18; 22-26 18-23; 26-31 27-24; 20-27 23-32.

On this occasion (Diagram 7) the winning method is ... 32-28; 26-30 28-24 (threatening 24-19); 16-20 18-23; 20-27 23-32. White wins.

In Diagram 8 White can force a favourable transposition to Diagram 6 after ... 6-10; 13-17 10-7 (forcing the black man on 11 onto the side of the board); 11-16 7-11; 16-20. White wins.

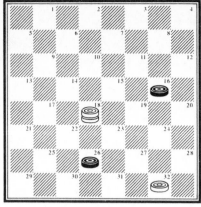

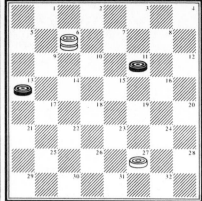

Diagram 7
White to move and win.

Diagram 8
White to move and win.

NOTE: Diagram 9 illustrates the important role of the dog-hole.

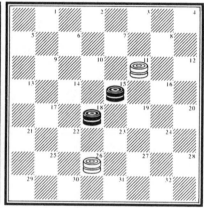

Diagram 9
White to move and win.

Diagram 10
White to move and win

White wins in Diagram 9 after ... 30-26; 21-25 26-22; 25-30 22-18; 30-25 28-32!; 19-24 (forced, otherwise White will capture this man, playing 32-27 and 18-15) 18-15; 25-22 15-19; 24-28 19-23.

NOTE: Diagrams 10-12 demonstrate the futility of memorising mountains of 'rules' regarding the opposition.

In Diagram 10 White wins after ... 26-22; 18-25 (or 15-8) 11-18. Here White had the opposition to start with, and retained it; neither capturing piece being removed from the board.

In Diagram 11 White wins after ... 11-15; 18-23 15-18; 23-27 (Black seems to be escaping) 21-17!; 9-13 (forced) 18-23; 13-22 23-32. Once again White had the opposition to start with and retained it.

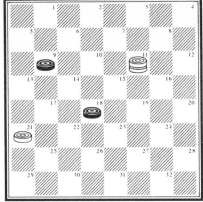
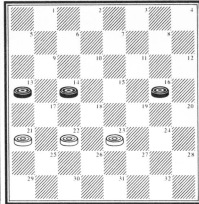

Diagram 11
White to move and win.

Diagram 12
White to move and draw

At the moment in Diagram 12 Black has the opposition. If White plays 22-18, Black will reply with 16-19, retaining the opposition, neither capturing piece being removed from the board, and win by First Position. However, ... 23-19!; 16-23 22-18; 23-26 (14-17 retains the opposition, but is pointless) 18-9; 26-31 9-6; 31-26 6-2; 26-23 2-6; 23-18 6-9 reverses the opposition and draws!

Exercises on the Opposition

 WARNING: Don't rely on 'rules' or 'systems'. Use your imagination, and give every move on the board consideration, no matter how ridiculous it seems at first glance.

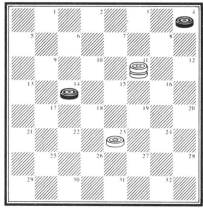

Exercise 1
White to move and win.

Exercise 2
White to move and win

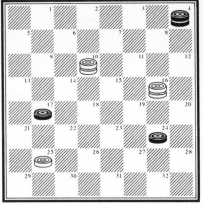 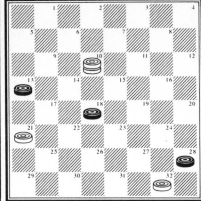

Exercise 3
White to move and win.

Exercise 4
White to move and win.

Summary

- Identify the key features of the situation.

- Try and get ahead in development.

- Position your kings judiciously.

- Be alert to the ways in which one king can hold two pieces.

- Recognise the winning potential afforded by a pivot man.

- Recognise the drawing potential afforded by a pivot man.

- Be aware of the strengths and weaknesses of a bridge.

- Learn the ideas embodied by the thirteen major endgame themes.

- Study problems to broaden the range of stratagems at your command.

Situations

In the endgame, planning is everything. The player must *firstly* make an accurate diagnosis of the situation, and *then* carry out a detailed analysis. Because they arise so frequently in play, a careful study of the 10 key situations which follow is vital. The training thus gained should also enable you to approach new situations more methodically.

Key Endgame 1: Payne's Single-Corner Win

Diagnosis

Force: 2 v 2. Opposition: Doesn't matter. Description: The white king on 26 stands guard over the black man on 21 and the black king on

25, until the other white piece, *which could be virtually anywhere on the board*, is ready to attack.

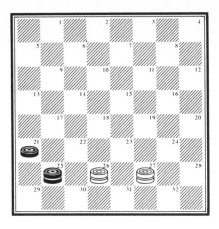

Diagram 13
Either to move: White wins

Analysis

Black to move: 25-29 27-23; 29-25 23-18; 25-29 18-22; 21-25 26-30. White wins.

White to move: ... 27-23; 25-29 23-18; 29-25 26-30; 25-29 18-22. White wins.

Key Endgame 2: The American Position

Diagram 14
White to move and win

Diagnosis

Force: 2 v 2. Opposition: White has it. Description: At the heart of the American Position is the confining nature of the single-corner zone: the fact that a king stationed in a single-corner square (4 and 29) has as little, or less, mobility than an uncrowned man anywhere on the board. Consequently, under the right conditions – and this includes possession of the opposition -, it is possible for 2 kings to defeat 2 connected opposing kings. The diagrammed setting, original with Dr T.J. Brown, represents a classic, early setting of the theme.

Analysis

... 3-7; 13-17 7-10 (of course 14-18 permits 17-22 and a draw); 17-22 14-18! (this is necessary; the natural 10-15 only draws); 22-25(A) 18-22; 25-29 (Black has now secured his 2 kings, but is still lost!) 22-26! (ready to play 26-30; 10-14 only draws); 21-25 26-30; 25-21 10-14; 29-25 14-18; 25-29 18-22. White wins.

A: Black has two options:

(i) 21-25 18-23; 25-21 10-14; 22-25 23-26; 25-29 26-30; 29-25 14-18; 25-29 18-22. White wins.

(ii) 22-26 10-14; 21-25 14-17; 25-21 17-22; 26-31 18-23. White wins.

The following additional settings should serve to clarify and generalise some of the fine points of this critical situation.

Setting A: Black kings on 25 and 29; white kings on 14 and 23. White to move; Black draws.

Setting B: Black kings on 25 and 29; white kings on 13 and 31. White to move; Black draws.

Setting C: Black kings on 29 and 30; white kings on 17 and 32. White to move and win.

Setting D: Black kings on 21 and 30; white kings on 5 and 26. White to move and win.

Settings A and B result in draws because, although possessing the opposition, White cannot get a king on 21 or 30 without allowing an exchange. In Setting C, White has a king ready to go to 21, and plays 32-27. The white king on 32 could just as effectively be on 15, 16, 24 or 31 (but not 14 because of the exchange); in other words two squares away from 23. In Setting D, White has a king ready to go to 30, and plays 5-9. The king on 5 could just as effectively be on 6, 7, 13 or 15 (but not 23 because of the exchange); in other words two squares away from 14.

Key Endgame 3: Payne's Double-Corner Draw

Diagnosis

Force: 3 v 2. Opposition: Black has it (ignore the pivot man on 5). Description: In order for Black to draw, it is vital that he can freely occupy squares 9 and 13 as required. His defence then consists of a perpetual see-saw movement between these two squares.

Diagram 15
Black to move and draw

Analysis

6-9 15-18; 9-13! (A) 18-22; 13-9 14-17; 9-13! (B) etc. Drawn.

A: 9-6? permits White to occupy square 13 with 14-17; 6-9 17-13; and results in a neat win after 9-6 18-22!; 6-2 13-9; 2-7 22-17; 7-10 17-13; 10-7 9-14; 7-2 13-9; 1-6 5-1; 6-13 14-9; 13-6 1-10. White wins.

B: Of course, 9-6? would lose as before after 17-13.

Key Endgame 4: Roger's Draw

Diagram 16
Black to move and draw

Diagnosis

Force: 3 v 2. Opposition: Black has it (ignore the pivot man on 13). Description: Black draws either by holding the white man on 13 or by permitting it to advance into 5 as the situation demands.

Analysis

1-6 16-11; 6-2!(A) 3-8; 2-6 8-12; 6-1 12-16; 1-6 16-19; 10-14 19-23; 6-10 23-26; 10-6 11-15; 6-1 15-19; 1-6 19-23; 6-10 26-22; 10-15 23-26; 15-10 26-30; 10-6 30-25; 6-10 25-21; 10-6 22-17; 6-10 etc. Drawn.

A: Black has no qualms about allowing White to enter the dog-hole with 13-9; 10-6 9-5; 6-1 3-7; 2-6 7-2; 6-9 11-15; 9-13 15-10; 13-9 etc. Drawn, as in Key Endgame Number 3.

NOTE: In an unequal endgame situation such as this, entering the dog-hole does not reverse the opposition: the pivot man is considered 'dead' wherever it is held.

Key Endgame 5: Howard's Draw

Diagram 17
Black to move and draw

Diagnosis

Force: 3 v 2. Opposition: Black has it (ignore the pivot man on 21). Description: As you would expect by now, Black draws by keeping the white kings at bay, while preventing the white man on 21 from ever advancing safely.

Analysis

14-9 11-16 (A); 9-14 16-19; 14-9 19-23; 10-14 (B) 1-5; 9-13 23-26; 14-18 5-1; 13-9 26-31 (C); 9-14 (D) etc. Drawn.

A: Of course, 21-17 permits 9-13 and a quick draw. Instead, White correctly attempts to bring his king on 11 into the action, via a round-about route.

B: 9-14 also draws here, but this is the simplest method, and is played with the occupation of square 13 in mind.

C: Again, 21-17 is met with 9-13 and an immediate draw.

D: There is simply no way in which White can make inroads into the black fortress.

Key Endgame 6: Fourth Position

Diagram 18
Black to move and draw

Diagnosis

Force: 4 v 3. Opposition: Black has it (ignore the pivot man on 12). Description: Having reached this stage, the draw virtually plays itself; Black simply moving his king on 2 to and fro. In effect, Black has an extra double-corner – formed by the men on 3 and 12 – and White has no means of either attacking the defending kings simultaneously or forcing an exchange. The skill, of course, lies in angling for this situation in advance; its early availability being indicated by the men on 3 and 12.

Analysis

2-6 11-15; 6-2 10-14; 2-6 14-9; 6-2 15-10; 2-7 etc. Drawn.

However, if White is to move, things are quite different. White has the opposition, and wins by means of a clever 'pitch' (the name sometimes given to the sacrifice of a piece): ... 11-15; 2-6 10-14; 1-5 15-18; 6-2 13-9; 5-1 9-5; 2-6 14-17; 6-2 17-13; 2-6 18-15; 6-2 15-10; 2-6 10-7!; 3-10 5-9; 6-2 9-6; 2-9 13-15. White wins. You will note that a similar idea was used in Chapter 3, Diagram 13.

Key Endgame 7: Payne's Single-Corner Draw

Diagram 19
Black to move and draw

Diagnosis

Force: 3 v 2. Opposition: Black has it (ignore the pivot man on 20). Description: Black draws by keeping the white kings at bay, while preventing the white man on 20 from ever advancing safely. Incidentally, it has been pointed out that should White try too hard to win this draw, he may well end up losing!

Analysis

7-10 19-16; 10-7 18-23; 11-8(A) 16-12; 8-11 23-19; 7-3(B) 12-16(C); 3-7 19-24; 11-15 24-28; 15-11 16-19; 7-3 28-32; 3-7(D)... Drawn.

A: This is cheeky, asking for 23-19? 8-12! and a black win. Instead of 11-8, 11-15 will also draw.

B: 7-10? fails after 19-16; 10-7 12-8!; 11-4 16-11; 7-16 20-11. White wins.

C: 19-16 asks for 3-7 and the win of Note B. Instead, Black replies with 11-15 16-19 (16-11 loses); 15-24 20-16. Drawn.

D: Black must be watchful. Instead, 3-8? loses after 20-16!; 11-20 19-24; 20-27 32-23. White wins.

Key Endgame 8: Third Position

Diagnosis

Force: 3 v 2. Opposition: Black has it (ignore the pivot man on 28). Description: The first thing to note is that if Black did not have the opposition on the two white kings, White would win easily. As it stands, however, White must exercise great caution; his main problem being to avoid drifting into Key Endgame Number 7. There are also two see-saw draws to avoid en route!

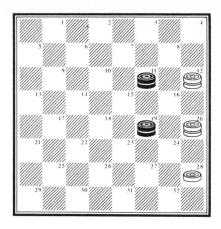

Diagram 20
White to move and win

Analysis

... 20-24; 11-15 24-27; 15-11 27-32(A); 11-15(B) 12-8; 15-18(C) 32-27(D); 19-16 27-31; 16-19 8-11; 18-23 11-7; 19-15 28-24(E); 23-27 24-20; 27-23 7-2; 23-19 2-6; 15-11 6-10(F); 11-8 31-26; 8-11 26-22; 11-8 22-18; 8-11 10-6(G); 11-7 6-9; 7-11 9-13!; 11-7 13-17; 7-11 17-21!; 11-7 21-25; 7-11 25-30(H); 19-24 18-23; 11-8 20-16; 24-20 16-12; 8-3 23-19; 20-16 19-15; 16-20 30-26; 20-16 26-23(I); 16-20 15-11; 20-24 23-18; 24-20 18-15; 20-24 11-16; 24-20 15-11; 20-24 16-20; 24-27 11-16; 27-32 20-24; 32-28 16-19; 28-32 24-28; 32-27 28-32; 27-31 19-15; 3-7 15-18; 7-11 18-22. White wins.

A: 27-31? permits See-Saw Draw Number 1, after 19-23 28-24; 23-27 24-20; 27-23 12-16; 11-15 16-12; 15-11 etc. Drawn.

B: 19-23 allows White to release the man on 28 immediately after 28-24; 11-15 32-28; 23-19 12-16; 19-12 24-19; 15-24 28-19. White wins.

C: 19-16 28-24; 16-12 24-19; 15-24 32-28; 12-3 28-19. White wins.

D: 8-11? permits See-Saw Draw Number 2, after 18-23 11-7; 19-16 7-10; 16-19 etc. Drawn.

E: 7-2 also wins, but this is highly instructive; leading into positions which may arise from other routes.

F: White establishes a king on 10. This prevents Black from moving 19-16 because of the threatened single exchange.

G: Now the phase of Third Position which is most likely to arise in play. White embarks on an elaborate journey with his king, designed to reach 30 without permitting Black to play 19-16 and the sanctuary of Payne's Single Corner Draw.

H: White has achieved his main goal, and can shortly start moving the man on 20.

I: White's plan is to completely immobilise the black king on 16.

WARNING: This is easily the hardest of the 10 Key Endgame Situations, but far tougher propositions exist!

Key Endgame 9: First Position

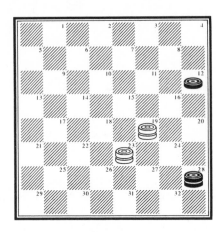

Diagram 21
White to move and win

Diagnosis

Force: 2 v 2. Opposition: White has it. Description: The diagrammed position represents a late, and critical, phase of First Position. The key features of this, the most important endgame situation in the game of draughts, are as follows:

1) At least one of Black's pieces is a single man.

2) White has, or can develop, two kings, while keeping Black's single man pinned to the right-hand side of the board. Typically, this man will initially be placed on square 3, 4 or 12. Of course, if it was placed on square 1 or 2, then it would have free access to White's left-hand side, and the situation would just be a draw.

3) Black's other piece, which becomes a king in the double-corner, is unable to reach the opposite double-corner.

White's winning procedure consists of attacking Black's king, immobilising it, and forcing Black's single man to advance into trouble. Black naturally tries to delay this advance for as long as possible.

Analysis

... 23-27; 28-32 19-23; 32-28 27-32; 28-24(A) 23-18 (of course 32-28 would permit the exchange with 24-19); 24-28(B) 18-15; 28-24 32-28; 24-27(C) 15-18; 12-16 (forced now, as 27-32 loses quickly after 18-23) 28-32; 27-24 18-15; 24-28 15-11!(D); 16-19 32-27; 28-32 27-31; 19-23 11-15; 32-28 15-19. White wins.

A: The early advance with 12-16 loses quickly after 32-27; 28-32 27-24; 16-20 24-28. White wins.

B: This is Black's most stubborn defence. However, White needs to master the three alternatives:

12-16 18-15; 16-20 15-18; 24-19 32-28; 19-16 18-23; 16-11 23-19; 11-8 28-32; 8-11 32-27; 11-8 27-23; 8-3 23-18 3-8 18-15; 8-12 15-11. White wins.

24-19 32-28; 12-16 28-32; 16-20 32-28; and the win above.

24-20 32-27; 20-16 18-15; 16-20 15-11; 12-16 11-15. White wins.

C: 24-20 15-11; 12-16 28-32; 16-19 11-15; 19-24 32-28; 24-27 28-32; 27-31 15-19. White wins.

D: Don't be tempted by 15-18?, as it allows a draw after 16-19 32-27; 19-23! (not 28-32?, which loses by 27-24!; 19-28 18-23) 27-32; 23-26. Drawn.

 WARNING: When the black man is initially on square 3 or 4, White must take care not to allow the black king to escape to join it, or a draw will result.

Key Endgame 10: Second Position

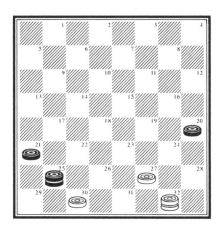

Diagram 22
White to move and win

Diagnosis

Force: 3 v 3. Opposition: White has it. Description: The features of this, arguably the second most important situation in the game, are as follows:

1) One of the black men is held on 21, and the other on the opposite side of the board.

2) The third black piece is, or can become, a king; although its scope is severely limited.

The winning procedure, though lengthy, is very mechanical, and consists of three phases:

1) Crowning three kings, while keeping the two black men pinned to the sides of the board.

2) Exchanging off the black king; changing the opposition in the process.

3) Exchanging off the black man on the right-hand side and regaining the opposition.

Analysis

... 32-28; 25-22 28-24; 22-18 24-19; 18-22 19-15; 22-17 15-18; 17-13 18-22 (the white king holds the man 21, so that his own man on 30 can be released); 13-9 30-26; 9-6 26-23; 6-10 23-18; 10-6 18-14; 6-1 14-9; 1-5 9-6; 5-1 6-2; 1-5 2-6; 5-1 6-10; 1-5 10-15; 5-9 15-19 (the white king now holds the man on 20, so that his own man on 27 can be released); 9-14 27-23; 14-10 23-18; 10-6 18-14; 6-1 14-9; 1-5 9-6; 5-1 6-2 (phase 1); 1-5 2-6; 5-1 6-10; 1-5 10-14; 5-1 14-18; 1-6 18-23; 6-10 23-27 (the king has to be brought back to this square); 10-14 19-23; 14-9 23-18; 9-6 18-14; 6-1 14-9; 1-5 22-17; 5-14 17-10 (phase 2); 21-25 10-15; 25-30 15-19; 30-26 27-32; 26-22 19-24; 20-27 32-23. White wins.

Summary

- Diagnosis before analysis!

- Payne's Single-Corner Win: one king holds two pieces in the single-corner, awaiting reserves.

- The American Position: two kings defeat two kings in the single-corner.

- Payne's Double-Corner Draw: man-down draw (pivot man on 5).

- Roger's Draw: man-down draw (pivot man on 13).

- Howard's Draw: man-down draw (pivot man on 21).

- Fourth Position: man-down draw (pivot man on 12).

- Payne's Single-Corner Draw: man-down draw (pivot man on 20).

- Third Position: won by avoiding Payne's Single-Corner Draw (pivot man on 28).

- First Position: 2 v 2 won by attacking the king and forcing the man to advance.

- Second Position: 3 v 3 won by crowning three kings and forcing two exchanges.

Themes

Many of the tactical devices given in Chapter 3 can be used at any stage of the game: it was purely for the sake of clarity that the examples and exercises were set with the minimum number of pieces. This section too is essentially tactical, but relates specifically to the endgame, and is subtler in nature. Too specific to be called situations, the themes given nonetheless have widespread applicability, and represent some of the ways by which experts execute a win (or draw).

TIP: When studying these themes, try and remember the ideas, not the positions!

1) Self-Destruct

This is the theme of using one of the opponent's men as a backstop.

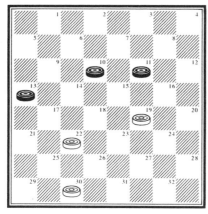 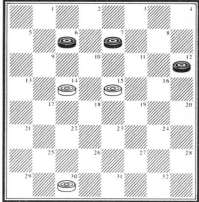

Diagram 23
White to move and win

Diagram 24
White to move and win

First of all, a reasonably straightforward example (Diagram 23). White wins after ... 22-18; 13-17 30-26!; 17-21 26-22; 21-25 18-15; 11-18 22-6.

Diagram 24 is very similar to the previous one. White wins after ... 30-26; 12-16 26-23!; 16-20 23-19; 20-24 15-10; 6-15 19-3.

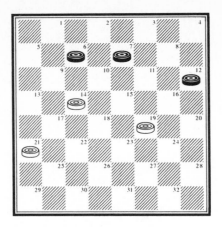

Diagram 25
White to move and win

In this example White wins after ... 19-15; 12-16 15-11; 6-10 11-2; 10-17 21-14.

2) Changing Guard

This is holding an opposing piece, first with a king, and then with a man, in order to win using the opposition.

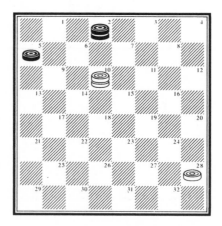

Diagram 26
White to move and win

A simple example. White wins after ... 28-24; 5-9 24-19; 9-13 19-15; 13-17 10-14!; 17-22 15-10!; 22-26 14-18.

3) Vice

This theme is using a king to grip the opponent's pieces in 'mid-air'.

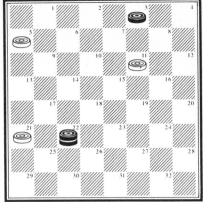

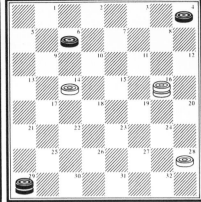

Diagram 27
White to move and win

Diagram 28
White to move and win

In Diagram 27 after ... 5-1; 22-18 1-6; 18-15 11-7!; 3-10 21-17 Black has no good move. White wins.

Diagram 28 is similar: ... 16-11; 4-8 11-4; 29-25 4-8; 25-22 8-11; 22-18 14-10!; 6-15 28-24. White wins.

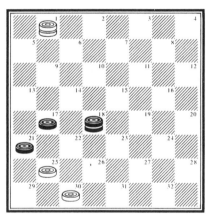

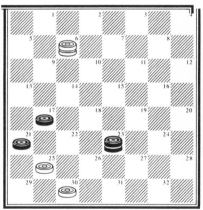

Diagram 29
White to move and draw

Diagram 30
White to move and draw

White looks to be in trouble in Diagram 29, but saves the day with ... 25-22!; 18-25 1-6; 25-22 6-9; 22-18 9-13; 18-22 13-9; 22-18 9-13; etc. Drawn.

Here's a similar example (Diagram 30). White draws after ... 30-26! (6-1 also draws –see Diagram 29); 23-30 6-9; 17-22 (30-26? loses to ... 9-13) 25-18.

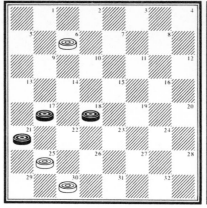

Diagram 31
White to move and draw

Diagram 32
White to move and draw

In Diagram 31 White once again sacrifices a man to draw after ... 25-22!; 18-25 6-1; 25-29 1-6; 29-25 6-9; 17-22 9-14; 22-26 30-23.

Despite having a man less, White can draw in Diagram 32 with ... 30-26!; 14-17 9-13; 18-22 26-23; 21-25 23-18; 22-15 13-29; 15-18 29-25.

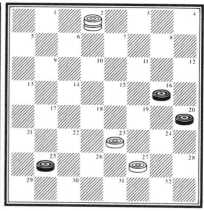

Diagram 33
Black to move, White wins

Diagram 34
White to move and win

In Diagram 33 Black has no way to avoid defeat: 27-23 (otherwise White gains the man on 9) 6-1; 23-14 1-5. White wins.

Diagram 34 features another similar example. White wins after ... 2-7; 25-30 7-11; 30-26 11-8; 26-19 8-12.

In Diagram 35 White can win with ... 23-18; 32-27 18-14; 27-31 14-9; 31-22 9-13.

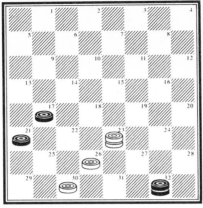 

Diagram 35
White to move and win

Diagram 36
White to move and win

In Diagram 36 White sets up a vice with ... 32-27!; 28-32 7-10; 32-23 10-14. White wins.

4) Pocket

This is the theme of forking a king and a man with the aid of one of your own men.

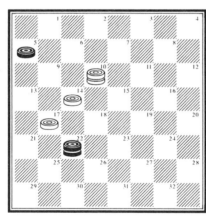 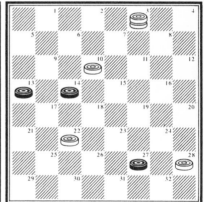

Diagram 37
White to move and win

Diagram 38
White to move and win

In Diagram 37 White has an extra man, but he is forced to give it up. However, he still wins after ... 17-13; 22-17 13-9; 17-13 10-6!; 13-17 14-10; 5-14 6-9; 14-18 9-14.

In Diagram 38 White wins after ... 3-7!; 27-31 7-2; 31-26 2-6; 26-17 6-9; 14-18 9-14. Charles Barker defeated James Reed in the 43rd game of their match in 1889 in this way.

Diagram 39
White to move and draw

White draws after ... 27-24!; 20-27 11-20; 26-19 20-24. I drew this in a practice game played against Harry Gibson in 1979.

5) Hanging Man

Leaving an opposing man 'high and dry'; that is, threatened with capture, and unable to escape.

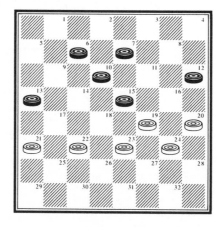

Diagram 40
White to move and win

In Diagram 40 White wins after ... 22-17!; 13-22 23-18; 7-11 18-14; 10-17 19-1. The black man on 17 is left 'high and dry'.

6) Single-Corner Block

This is jamming your opponent's pieces in the single-corner zone.

Diagram 41
White to move and win

Diagram 42
White to move and win

In Diagram 41 White jams his opponent's pieces into a single-corner and wins with ... 31-26; 10-3 26-22!; 18-25 16-11.

In Diagram 42 White wins with ... 27-23!; 19-26 18-14!; 10-17 29-25.

7) Double-Corner Block

This occurs when you jam the opponent's pieces in the double-corner.

Diagram 43
White to move and win

Diagram 44
White to move and win

In Diagram 43 White blocks Black in the double-corner after ... 32-27!; 28-32 27-24!; 19-28 26-23. White wins.

In Diagram 44 White wins after ... 19-16!; 12-19 11-16; 24-28 31-27; 23-32 16-23. Tom Wiswell defeated Millard Hopper in the 14th game of their match in 1951 in this way.

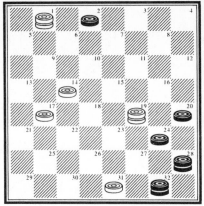

Diagram 45
White to move and win

Diagram 46
White to move and win

In Diagram 45 White wins after ... 1-6!; 2-18 19-23; 18-27 17-13 (or 17-14). James Ferrie defeated a very surprised James Moir like this!

Diagram 46 is another similar example. White wins with ... 19-24; 27-32 13-17!; 20-27 17-22.

8) Squeeze

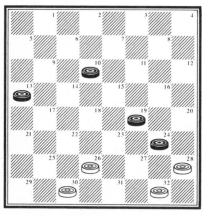
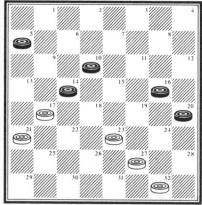

Diagram 47
White to move and win

Diagram 48
White to move and win

A squeeze is a press from the front, using another man or the edge of the board.

In this first example (Diagram 47) White wins after ... 26-23!; 19-26 30-23; 24-27 23-18; 27-31 32-27; 31-24 28-19; 13-17 18-14.

In Diagram 48 White wins similarly with ... 23-18!; 14-23 27-18; 20-24

32-28; 24-27 28-24; 27-31 24-20; 16-19 18-15.

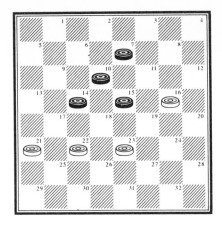

Diagram 49
White to move and draw

... 21-17!; 14-21 23-18; 15-19 18-15; 10-14 22-17; 14-18 17-14; 21-25 (say) 15-11 (or 15-10) and White draws. Jack Botte drew this against Tom Wiswell in their 1973 match.

9) Steal

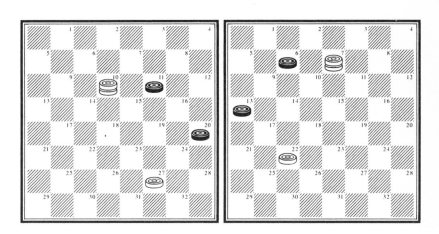

Diagram 50
White to move and win

Diagram 51
White to move and win

A steal is winning a man by means of a squeeze.

In this first example (Diagram 50) White wins after ... 27-23!; 20-24 (11-16 loses to 10-15) 23-19!; 11-15 10-14.

In Diagram 51 White wins with ... 22-18!; 13-17 (6-9 loses to 7-10) 18-14!; 6-10 7-11.

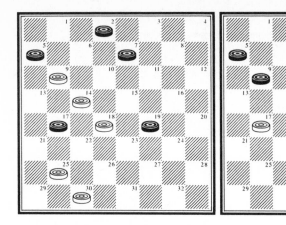

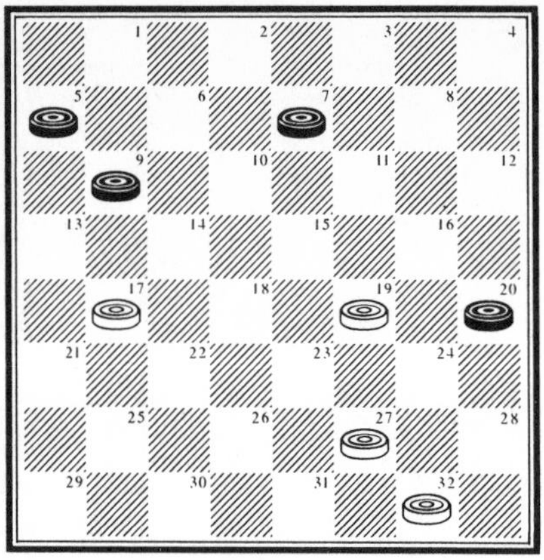

Diagram 52
White to move and win

Diagram 53
White to move and win

In this example (Diagram 52) White wins after sacrificing a man with ... 9-6!; 2-9 25-22; 17-26 30-16; 9-13 18-15; 13-17 15-11!.

Another win with a steal (Diagram 53): ... 19-15!; 9-13 17-14; 13-17 27-24 (or 27-23); 20-27 32-23; 17-22 23-19; 22-26 19-16; 26-31 15-11! and White wins.

10) Nipped at the Wire

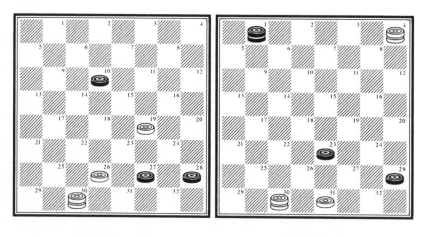

Diagram 54
White to move and win

Diagram 55
White to move and win

This theme is winning by means of a reverse 2 for 2.

In this first example (Diagram 54) White wins with ... 19-15!; 10-19 26-23; 19-26 30-32.

In this more complex example (Diagram 55) White wins after ... 4-8;

1-6 8-11; 6-10 31-26!; 23-27 11-15; 10-19 26-23; 19-26 30-32.

Diagram 56
White to move and win

Here White has two kings to none, but the winning process is still difficult. White wins after ... 28-32; 20-24 32-28; 24-27 28-24; 27-32 24-19; 32-27 30-25!; 22-26 19-23; 27-18 25-22; 18-25 29-31.

11) Captive Cossacks

This theme is blocking a man which is just about to crown.

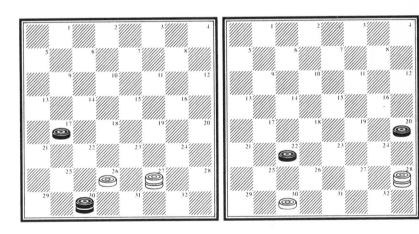

Diagram 57
White to move and win

Diagram 58
White to move and win

Diagram 57 is fairly straightforward. White wins after ... 26-22!; 17-26 27-31; 30-25 31-29.

Similarly, White wins here (Diagram 58) after ... 28-32; 20-24 32-28; 24-27 30-26!; 22-31 28-32; 31-26 32-30.

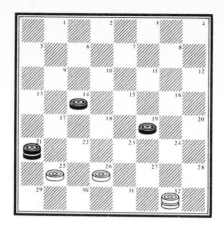

Diagram 59
White to move and draw

In this example White escapes with a draw after ... 26-23!; 19-26 32-27; 21-30 27-31; 14-17 (or 30-25, but not 14-18?) 31-13.

12) Ace in the Hole

Threatening a 2 for 1 which cannot be avoided.

Diagram 60
White to move and win

Diagram 61
White to move and draw

We start with a simple example (Diagram 60). Here White wins with ... 20-16!.

Hugh Henderson lost against George Buchanan with 10-15? here in the 1905 Scottish Open Championship (Diagram 61). Instead White can draw with ... 22-17!; 31-22 10-15; 9-14 17-10.

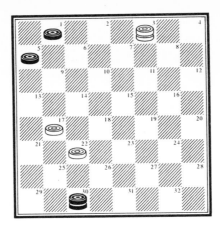

Diagram 62
White to move and draw

White looks to be in some difficulty here, but a draw can be obtained after ... 17-13; 30-25 22-17; 25-21 13-9!; 21-14 3-7; 1-6 9-2.

13) Hobson's Choice

This is a subtler version of Optional Jumps and is often used to obtain a man-down draw.

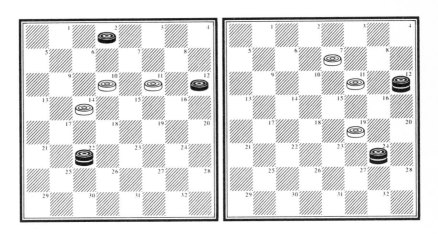

Diagram 63
White to move and draw

Diagram 64
White to move and win

In Diagram 63 White can force a draw with ... 14-9; 22-18 9-5!; 18-15 11-7!; 2-11 5-1; 15-6 1-10; 11-16 10-15; 16-20 15-19.

In Diagram 64 White wins after ... 19-15; 24-19 15-10; 19-15 11-8!; 12-3 7-2; 15-6 2-9 (White has the opposition).

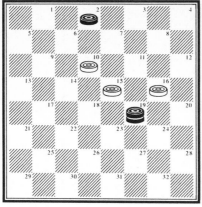

Diagram 65
White to move and win

Diagram 66
White to move and draw

In Diagram 65 White can win with the following sequence: ... 16-11; 19-16 10-7; 16-19 15-10; 19-15 10-6!; 2-9 7-3; 15-8 3-12.

Despite having 3 men against 3 kings, White can draw in Diagram 66 with ... 15-10!; 19-12 6-2; 14-7 2-11.

Exercises

TIP: When tackling the examples, I would again advise you to take no longer than three minutes over each one, before referring to the solution (if required).

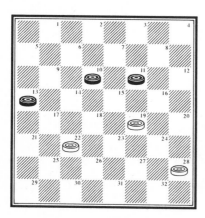
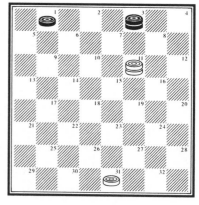

Exercise 5: Self-Destruct
White to move and win

Exercise 6: Changing Guard
White to move and win

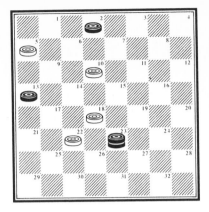

Exercise 7: Vice
White to move and win

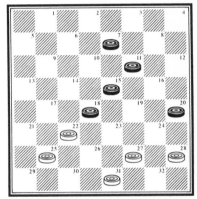

Exercise 8: Vice
White to move and win

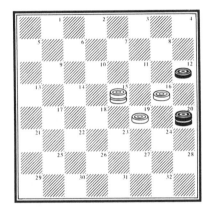

Exercise 9: Pocket
White to move and win

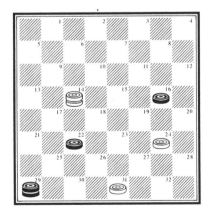

Exercise 10: Hanging Man
White to move and win

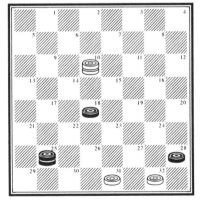

Exercise 11: Single-Corner Block
White to move and win

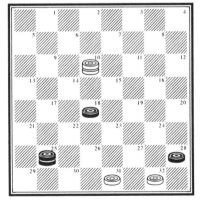

Ex 12: Double-Corner Block
White to move and win

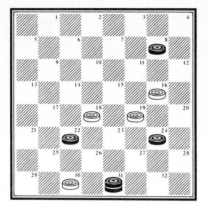

Exercise 13: Squeeze
White to move and win

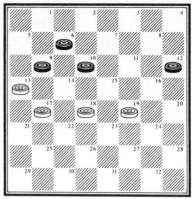

Exercise 14: Steal
White to move and win

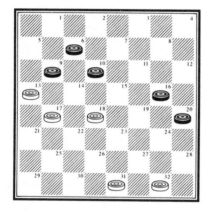

Exercise 15: Steal
White to move and win

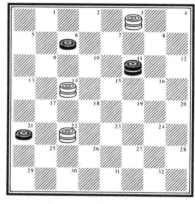

Exercise 16: Nipped At The wire
White to move and win

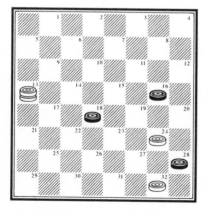

Exercise 17: Captive Cossacks
White to move and win

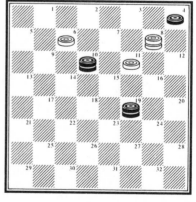

Exercise 18: Ace In The Hole
White to move and draw

 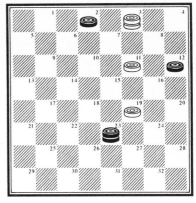

Exercise 19: Hobson's Choice
White to move and draw

Exercise 20: Hobson's Choice
White to move and draw

Summary

- Themes are essentially endgame tactics.

- The thirteen themes given are frequently used by experts to register wins (and draws).

- Each theme embodies a particular idea. Learn the ideas, not the positions.

Chapter Five

The Midgame

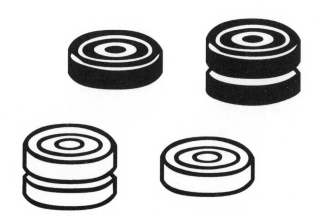

Introduction

Definition: 'The midgame begins as a result of carrying out one of a huge variety of 'waiting' or preliminary combinations (the opening). In the midgame, schemes of attack and defence, with one or more objectives, are initiated and carried to a 'climactic point', after which the action assumes a declining role of importance.' (Maurice Chamblee)

'The climactic, or critical, point is reached when the defender has completed his defensive combination or, in cases where the defence has been unsuccessful, the attacker has completed his winning combination. After this climactic point is reached, the midgame structures begin to 'melt away', [sometimes] leading to the phase known as the endgame. The early midgame, regarded by almost all the top players as the most important phase of development in the entire game, leads from the opening up to the climactic point, while the late midgame leads from the climactic point to the endgame.' (Maurice Chamblee)

The midgame, dubbed the 'muddle game' by Tom Wiswell, rarely receives methodical treatment in the literature, leaving the reader to infer things for himself from a vast array of master – and sometimes deeply flawed (!) – games. While it is impossible to generalise with complete safety – 'Ultimately it is the position of every piece on the board which counts' (Walter Hellman) – there are many useful principles which can be applied to the midgame with good effect. Attempting to bypass the issue by dint of a parrot-like memory and 'brute-force' visualisation is futile.

 TIP 1: Try and gain at least equal control of the centre.

The centre, represented by squares 14, 15, 18, and 19 plays a vital part in every game, and a number of approaches may be made to gain its control:

1) Occupying one or more of the central squares;

2) Allowing your opponent to occupy these squares, and attempting to grip his men by means of a pincer movement;

3) Leaving these squares vacant, and contesting their control by means of men posted on 17, 22, 23 and 24 (from Black's viewpoint, 16, 11, 10 and 9).

Moreover, when an opportunity presents itself to 'take the centre', by playing the move 22-18 (11-15 for Black) before your opponent can play the counter-part 11-15, you should generally take it.

Here, White plays too passively, totally neglecting the centre, allowing Black to gain complete control by means of occupation.

11-15 22-17; 15-19 24-15; 10-19 23-16; 12-19 25-22; 8-11 17-13?; 9-14 22-17?; 7-10 27-24?; 11-15 32-27; 4-8 29-25; 8-11 25-22; 3-8 26-23; 19-

26 30-23; 15-18 22-15; 10-26 31-22; 14-18 22-15; 11-18. Black wins.

Black's winning method consists of crowning the man on 18, returning it to 22, exchanging with 6-9, jumping 22-13 and leaving the white man on 6 high and dry.

In the next case, Black overcrowds the centre with his own men, and White carries out a crushing pincer attack.

11-15 23-19; 8-11 22-17; 4-8 25-22; 9-14? 17-13; 14-18? 29-25; 5-9? 26-23; 9-14 22-17; 1-5 30-26; 5-9 26-22. White wins.

In summary, you should always try and obtain at least an equal share of the centre, but retain mobility by not overcrowding it with your own men.

TIP 2: Don't underestimate the value of side moves.

It is *generally preferable* to move towards the centre, since there, a man is able to move in two directions. However, though limited to moving in just one direction, this does not mean, as some hacks would have it, that a man on the side is invariably weak:

1) It is immune from capture;

2) A white man on 13 can be used either to support an advanced man on 9 or, in conjunction with one on 18, may impose a severe 'cramp' – restriction of mobility – on Black's double-corner.

3) Likewise, a white man on 20 can be used either to support a man which has infiltrated on 16 or, in conjunction with one on 18, may impose a severe cramp on Black's single-corner.

TIP 3: Develop your single-corner men early.

Generally speaking, the men which occupy your single-corner (squares 21, 22, 25 and 29 for White) should be developed rapidly. This is because, since there is only one entry square to the king-row, this area of the board is less vulnerable to attack than the double-corner. You can easily convince yourself of this by setting up the men for the start of a game, and removing those in the single-corners. Consequently, the sequence 21-17 and 17-13 is very common: two good developing moves which leave the body of White's forces intact, and impose a slight cramp on Black's double-corner.

TIP 4: Protect your double-corner.

In general, you should try and retain as much strength as possible in your double-corner (squares 24, 27, 28 and 32 for White). Reason: set up the men for the start of a game, remove those in the double-corners, and you will see how easy it is to enter the king-row. 'A player with a strong double-corner is doubly hard to corner.' (Tom Wiswell)

TIP 5: Try and keep your position intact.

Creating unnecessary 'holes' in your position, as in the following example, is bad policy, and tends to lead to a ragged game, which a skilful opponent can exploit.

11-16 22-18; 16-20 24-19; 7-11?(A) 18-15!(B); 11-18 23-7; 3-10 to a probable White win.

A: This is horrible, 8-11 being best, since it allows White to break up Black's position, and gains nothing in return. Once your position has been disrupted in this way, it is almost impossible to patch it up again without making major concessions in other areas such as time and force.

B: 19-15 and 19-16 are also very powerful.

Other aspects of intactness also merit careful attention:

1) Unless there is a specific reason for doing so, *and notable counter-examples do exist*, you should avoid moving the man on 26 (7 for Black) – known as the 'apex' man – early in the game.

2) When your opponent has a man on 15 it is often wise to exchange it off, replacing it with one of your own men. In line with Tips 3 and 4, 22-18; 15-22 25-18 is generally preferred over 24-19; 15-24 28-19 for this purpose. Exchanging off a man on 14 with 23-18; 14-23 27-18 or 23-18; 14-23 26-19 is more radical, particularly in the early stages of the game, and should only be done with a definite objective in mind. This applies even more so to the removal of a man on 16 with 23-19; 16-23 27-18 or 23-19; 16-23 26-19.

NOTE: Although there are instances of side jumps such as 26-17 and 27-20 being sound, or even essential, it is best, as a general rule, to jump towards the centre.

3) You should be completely flexible regarding the movement of the men in your king-row! Most beginners make it a rule to avoid moving these men until forced to do so, but this is mistaken. Certainly the king-row needs protection, but typically the retention of two men, or even one man (usually 31 or 30 for White), is perfectly adequate for the purpose, leaving 10 men in the 'outfield' to fight the battle. The question of which two men to retain depends entirely upon the demands of the particular development or formation in question, but the following pointers may help:

a) Circumstances permitting, the man on 29 is usually developed early on, in line with the principle of rapid single-corner development.

b) Retaining two men on 30 and 32 and, to a lesser extent, two men on 29 and 31, *can be effective*, often leading to involved bridge endgames. However, the early movement of the man on 31 sometimes creates a dangerous elbow.

c) Retaining two men on 30 and 31, in conjunction with the apex man on 26, forms a very sturdy defensive structure, and allows for the immediate trading off of a man crowning on 32. This particular configuration often arises out of a 'pyramid' formation (see Early Midgame Formations).

d) Retaining two men on 31 and 32, often seen in a 'long dyke' formation (see Early Midgame Formations), lends considerable weight to the double-corner, and allows White to freely develop all the men on his left-hand side.

In summary, 'Moves which disturb your position the least, disturb your opponent the most!' (Tom Wiswell)

TIP 6: Don't overdevelop your men.

If your men have, taken as a whole, made further progress up the board than your opponent's then, as was discussed in the introduction to the endgame, you are said to be ahead in development. While this is an advantage in the late midgame and endgame, unless you have access to your opponent's king-row it is a disadvantage – *and sometimes a fatal one!* – in the opening and early midgame. This is because many formations, most notably the long dyke, depend upon having a reserve of 'waiting' moves in order to survive onslaughts from the opponent. Therefore, you should *encourage* your opponent to make exchanges which 'gain' time, while avoiding them yourself.

TIP 7: Be aware of the power of waiting moves.

The element of time is multifaceted, three aspects being the opposition, gaining a tempo and the relative state of development of the opposing forces. Waiting moves represent the fourth aspect, and their potency is often overlooked. All moves in draughts may be roughly classified into three categories: the objective move; the developing move (such as moving along the single-corner diagonal) – usually made to support an objective; the waiting move – a timing move by which an objective or developing move is carried through.

'Timing is the 'fourth dimension' of draughts, and only by a patient study of its usage and importance can the student hope to become an adept of the art.' (Willie Ryan)

TIP 8: Become familiar with the six major midgame formations (see Early Midgame Formations).

The midgame largely operates in the element of space, and is fundamentally about formations – their construction and maintenance. It is impossible to reach a high standard without developing an intuitive feel for what is or is not in keeping with a given formation.

TIP 9: Become familiar with the value of individual squares.

Mainly because of their virtual immobility, squares 5 and 12 should generally be avoided by White. Conversely, given adequate support, it is usually advantageous for White to invade/infiltrate on squares 9, 10, 11 and 16, because of the disruptive effect on Black's position. The occupation of square 14 often signals an attack on the double-corner – easier to attack than the single-corner – classically seen in dyke formations, *but needs support in order to be effective.*

TIP 10: Given a 'secure' king-row, look for opportunities to 'sacrifice' a man in order to get a 'free king'.

Clearly a little elaboration is required:

'Secure': The king-row is sufficiently well guarded that your opponent will have to return at least one man in order to break through. It does not necessarily require all four men to be in place.

'Sacrifice': Giving up material on positional grounds, with a (likely) view to regaining it, preferably with interest, in the future. Simple tactical devices, where the material given up is regained immediately, do not represent genuine sacrifices.

WARNING: Sacrificing *two* men in order to get a free king is very rarely justified, and has led to several losses among top-ranking players.

'Free king': A king, generally crowned in the double-corner, which has considerable freedom of movement, and can harass your opponent's men from behind; particularly effective when they are bunched in the centre of the board. Inexperienced players, in particular, tend to feel jittery when a king is breathing down their neck in this way – computer programs don't! – and often miss the best defence.

WARNING: A king which is stuck in the single-corner, typically as the result of an in-and-out shot, may be more of a liability than an asset.

WARNING: If your opponent sacrifices a man, it is always wise to decide *immediately* whether you think he has blundered or played a brilliancy. If the latter, you should try and evaluate the most opportune moment for returning it. Many a game has been lost where a player tried to hold on to his extra material for too long.

TIP 11: Use the process of elimination, especially when in a weak position.

In the midgame elimination is used almost sub-consciously by experts, eliminating first those moves which lead to the immediate loss of material (fairly easy to do), and then those which are strategically awful (less easy). Attention is then given to the subset of remaining moves which are in tune with the needs of the position (candidate moves), and finally to the move to be played. Here, powers of visualisation (see Early Midgame Formations) are brought strongly to bear; a judgement (static evaluation) being made at the point where the player can't 'see' any further. However, the main role of elimination is in the discarding of clear-cut losing moves when defending a weak position; the reasoning being that it is better to play a move which *might* lose (can't tell) than one which *does* lose. Similarly, in a strong position, elimination is used to discard moves which permit your opponent clear-cut draws; it being better to play a move which *might* win (can't tell) than one which *doesn't* win. Obviously the process is not foolproof but used efficiently, is very powerful.

 TIP 12: After your opponent has moved, look with particular care at the new move(s) which is available to you. You will be surprised how often this pays dividends.

 TIP 13: When your opponent has created a weakness in your position, rather than necessarily attend to it, see if there is profit in creating a counter-weakness (computers are excellent at this!).

 TIP 14: In many of your games you will work long and hard to establish a man on a strong square, don't move it without a good reason!

 TIP 15: Keep your options open: don't commit a man to a particular square unnecessarily early.

Summary

- Try and gain at least equal control of the centre.
- Don't underestimate the value of side moves.
- Develop your single-corner men early.
- Protect your double-corner.
- Try and keep your position intact.
- Don't overdevelop your men.
- Be aware of the power of waiting moves.
- Become familiar with the six major midgame formations.
- Become familiar with the value of individual squares.
- Look for opportunities to sacrifice a man in order to get a free king.
- Use the process of elimination.
- Look carefully at the new move(s) available to you on each turn.
- Create counter-weaknesses!
- Don't move a good man without good reason!
- Keep your options open.

Late Midgame Classics

Just as there are key endgame situations which must be mastered, so there are many classic late midgame positions. The four given here crop up with the greatest frequency, and therefore warrant close attention. In order of importance they are: Fifth Position, Lucas' Position, Cowan's Coup and Strickland's Draw.

Mastery of these positions depends upon the following:

1) Memorising the positions;

2) Understanding the continuations;

3) Angling for them (or avoiding them!) at an early stage.

Classic Late Midgame Position 1: Fifth Position

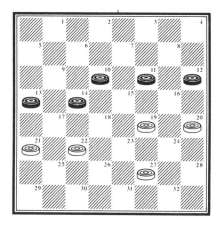

Diagram 1
White to move and draw

Solution: ... 20-16! (Black was threatening 11-15); 11-20 27-23; 20-24 22-18; 24-27 18-9; 10-14 (if 27-31, then 23-18; 10-14 18-15; 31-27 15-11; 27-23 19-15; 23-19 15-10 and a draw; thanks to the supporting black man on 13) 9-6; 27-31 6-2; 31-27 2-6; 27-18 6-9; 13-17 19-15; 18-11 9-18; 17-22 18-25; 11-15 25-22! Drawn. At the last move, 21-17? would lose by 15-18!.

Classic Late Midgame Position 2: Lucas' Position

Solution: ... 20-16!; 11-20 18-15; 20-24 15-6; 24-27 6-2; 27-31 2-6; 31-27 6-13; 27-18 13-9. White wins.

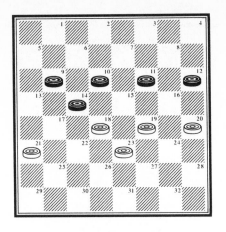

Diagram 2
White to move and win

Classic Late Midgame Position 3: Cowan's Coup

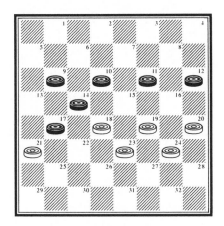

Diagram 3
White to move and draw

Solution: ... 19-16!; 12-28 (if 12-26, then 24-19; 14-23 21-7; 26-31 7-3; 31-27 3-8. Drawn.) 23-19; 14-23 21-7; 28-32 7-3; 32-27 3-8. Drawn.

Classic Late Midgame Position 4: Strickland's Draw

Solution: ... 23-18!; 14-23 27-18; 16-23 24-19; 20-24 (if 11-16, then 31-27; 7-11 21-17; 23-26 18-14; 16-23 14-7! Drawn); 21-17!; 24-28 17-13!; 11-16 31-27; 7-11 19-15!; 10-19 27-24. Drawn.

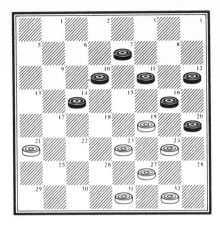

Diagram 4
White to move and draw

NOTE: Needless to say, like virtually everything else in this book, all these positions can arise with colours reversed.

TIP: In a late midgame position, on your move, the simplest way to see if any of the above positions is attainable – assuming no exchanges are required – is to count up the number of moves needed to get each set of forces onto the desired squares. If the numbers match, then the position is *possible.* Whether or not it is *probable,* or *desirable,* is then a matter for your analysis.

Summary

● The four most important late midgame positions are Fifth Position (5 by 5), Lucas' Position (5 by 5), Cowan's Coup (6 by 6) and Strickland's Draw (7 by 7).

● It is important to memorise these positions, understand their continuations and be able to angle for them (or avoid them) at an early stage.

● Checking whether a particular position is *possible,* is best done by mentally moving, en bloc, both sets of forces onto the desired squares, and counting the number of moves required.

Early Midgame Formations

In the early midgame there are six particular configurations of men – patterns or *formations* – which are both effective and of frequent occurrence:

1) The dyke formation (long and short);

2) The pyramid formation;

3) The phalanx formation;

4) The mill formation;

5) The echelon formation;

6) The mixed formation.

Sometimes, rather than attempting to create these patterns, you will seek to frustrate the efforts of your opponent, and sometimes, where both of you adopt preventative measures, no distinguishable pattern will appear at all. Clearly though, in all cases an understanding of formations is required. This understanding, while in no way providing a blanket coverage of the early midgame, will enable you in many instances to select appropriate developing and waiting moves. 'Analysis' of the 'If I go here, and he goes there, and I go here...' sort, simply won't stand up.

Formation Number 1A: The Long Dyke

Screening out all the other men, a fully developed long dyke formation looks like this:

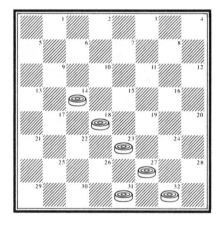

Diagram 1
A fully developed long dyke formation

The long dyke is essentially an aggressive formation for three reasons:

It is directed towards the opponent's double-corner;

It establishes a man on the 5th row;

It is created along the A-line, and precludes the opponent from doing the same.

 NOTE: The men on 31 and 32 are particularly important. While forming no part of the line, the man on 31 is, of course, immune

from being jumped, and strengthens the whole structure. The man on 32 is similarly immune, and is the base upon which the entire line rests. Moving it early on invariably results in a weakness which the opponent can attack, and is not recommended unless there is no decent alternative.

The intention of the dyking player is to maintain the formation throughout the early midgame, dominating the centre and forcing the opponent on to inferior squares at the side of the board.

Formation Number 1B: The Short Dyke

Screening out all the other men, a fully developed short dyke formation looks like this:

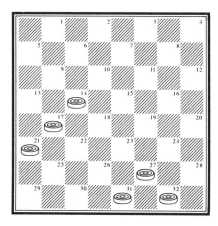

Diagram 2
A fully developed short dyke formation

NOTE: It is the three men on 14, 17 and 21 (12, 16 and 19 for Black) which give the short dyke its name, but those on 27, 31 and 32 are invaluable if infiltrating enemy men are to be intercepted.

While the value of the long dyke is appreciated by players of all standards, the short dyke tends to be a rather underestimated weapon. It has several good points:

1) Requiring only a line of three men, as opposed to five, the short dyke is easier to erect than the long.

2) In contrast to the long dyke, the short can usually be created without incurring commitments in time-count.

'A considerable amount of co-operation from a weak opponent is needed to create a long dyke yet be on a level time-count.' (Derek Oldbury)

3) It threatens to advance, or exchange, into 10.

4) It threatens, on being blocked from occupying 10 by the move 6-10, to create twin outposts on 13 and 14 by means of the exchange 17-13; 10-17 21-14. These will intimidate Black's double corner, and removing them with a 2 for 1 (either 6-9 13-6; 2-18 or 6-9 13-6; 1-17, depending on whether 1-6 or 2-6 has been played earlier) will be met with a 2 for 1 in return; often resulting in weaknesses in the black position in the late midgame.

5) It can be an effective counter (anti-formation) to a long dyke.

Formation Number 2: The Pyramid

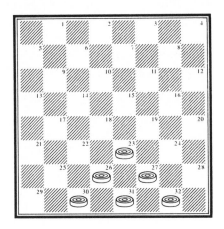

Diagram 3
A fully developed pyramid formation

Screening out all the other men, a fully developed pyramid formation looks like the example in Diagram 3:

Actually a triangle, but popularly known as a pyramid to emphasise its solidity, several points can be made about this formation:

1) It exists at the start of the game, and so does not need to be set up: it's already fully developed!

2) It can be of great defensive value.

3) Being essentially passive – it only reaches the 3rd row, whereas the dyke, phalanx and mill, which are active patterns, reach the 5th row, and the echelon, which is semi-active, reaches the 4th row – it is often opposed by another pyramid, or echelon, and the resulting play tends to be rather limited in scope.

4) Its underlying principle is to 'sit tight' for as long as possible, keeping the pyramid intact, and make moves with the other men; latterly reducing the pyramid to the three men on 26 (apex man), 30 and 31. Draughts not being static, you will obviously be forced to break it at some point!

Formation Number 3: The Phalanx

Screening out all the other men, a fully developed phalanx formation looks like this:

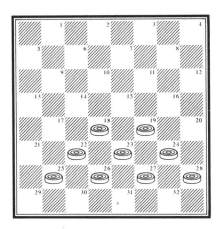

Diagram 4
A fully develop phalanx formation

Three key points need to be noted:

1) Obviously one or two men are required in the king-row in order to give the formation some support. Their precise positions will depend upon the opening in question.

2) Notice how the white men have closed up behind each other, without leaving any 'holes'.

3) Though it looks imposing, and may indeed be powerful, when handling the phalanx you should always be wary of a pincer movement by your opponent: it is all too easy to overcrowd the centre!

Formation Number 4: The Mill

Screening out all the other men, a fully developed mill formation looks like the example in Diagram 5:

The motivation behind this formation is as follows:

1) To establish, usually by means of an exchange, an 'outpost' man on 15 (18 for Black) – see also Squares.

2) To use this outpost as a spearhead, by developing twin segments of three men on 25, 22 and 18, and 28, 24 and 19 respectively.

3) It is usually difficult for the opponent to dislodge the outpost man without damaging his position.

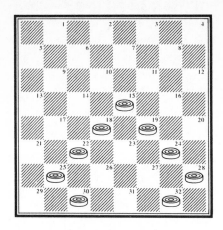

Diagram 5
A fully developed mill formation

TIP: Don't dismiss the opportunity to develop just one of these segments, as it may still be effective.

WARNING: It is essential that the outpost man has adequate support, that is, does not occupy 15 prematurely, or it will become a liability rather than an asset. Moreover, like the phalanx, it is crucial when handling the mill not to allow your opponent to use a pincer movement to bind your men in the centre.

Formation Number 5: The Echelon

Screening out all the other men, a fully developed echelon formation looks *something* like the example in Diagram 6:

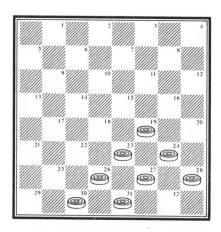

Diagram 6
A fully developed echelon formation

The echelon takes a variety of forms, but the following general points can be made:

1) It usually comprises several lines of men, arranged in parallel, each with its leader clear of the one in front in order to retain a degree of mobility.

2) It often incorporates the waiting move 32-27 (1-6 for Black), which can be withheld for use at a suitable point.

3) It often involves the establishment of a supported man on 16 (17 for Black)

4) Being only semi-active, it can be opposed by pincers, a pyramid or another echelon.

Formation Number 6: The Mixed

Usually created when one side's dyke outpost is countered by the other side's mill outpost – although other combinations exist – a typical mixed formation is shown below:

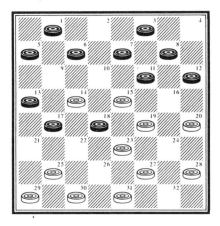

Diagram 7
A typical mixed formation

Willie Ryan characterised the mixed formation as positions in which the men are 'entangled in complete confusion', noting that James Reed, who was 'unbeatable when sober' (!), was a master of 'chop suey checkers', who would often lead his opponents into 'a maze of complications so dense that they became hopelessly lost in their kaleidoscopic patterns.'

NOTE: Though some may question the use of the word 'formation' in this instance, these positions are of such frequent occurrence that they are worthy of separate study.

WARNING: In highly complex positions it is often very dangerous to attempt simplification; the only 'safe' course being to complicate further.

TIP: Because there are so many 'contact points' between the opposing forces, tactical considerations run high in the mixed formation. The solving of advanced tactical problems, is therefore crucial in order to develop the necessary armoury and visualisation skills.

Visualisation Pointers

1) When you feel you've looked ahead as far as you can, make yourself look one move further!

2) Try and solve problems without physically moving the pieces.

3) Use the numbers of the squares to aid in recalling where particular pieces are during your analysis. (Incidentally, boards used in competition don't normally have the numbers on them.)

4) Picture only the 32 playing squares rather than the whole board. It's much simpler!

5) 'Move' the pieces into their new positions rather than carry out jumps in your head.

6) Use a simple scoring system to ensure you are getting a fair deal. For example, 'I give up a man (0-1), take 2 (2-1), he takes 1 (2-2), I give up another (2-3), I take 2 more (4-3) and he finishes the sequence by taking 1 (4-4). Fair!' Even the greatest players have been guilty of miscounting at times!

7) Half close your eyes to permit partial retention of the current position while 'looking' at new ones.

8) Remember that the ability to follow a given sequence of moves in your head is a purely technical skill: you have to combine visualisation with understanding if you wish to succeed.

9) Bear in mind that draughts is not primarily a test of how far ahead you can look: in many cases the question isn't even meaningful.

NOTE: It is much easier to visualise on a colourless board than a chequered one!

The very antithesis of the mixed formation, worthy of mention, is the open game. Here the forces are almost entirely disentangled – virtually no contact points – and the basic strategy is to make non-committal waiting moves; taking care not to advance any man to a square where it might become a liability.

WARNING: Although having strongly drawish tendencies, this anti-formational approach is still productive of wins in the hands of its leading exponents. Therefore, never relax!

Summary

● An understanding of the six recurring formations is essential if you wish to make sense of many of the early midgame manoeuvres.

● The mixed formation, alone, is overtly tactical, and largely a test of visualisation.

Chapter Six

The Opening

- 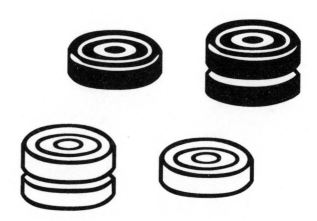 Introduction
- Ballots

Introduction

Definition: 'The opening is an initial combination of moves, fully executed, resulting in the achievement of definite, complete, preliminary objectives by both sides.' (Maurice Chamblee)

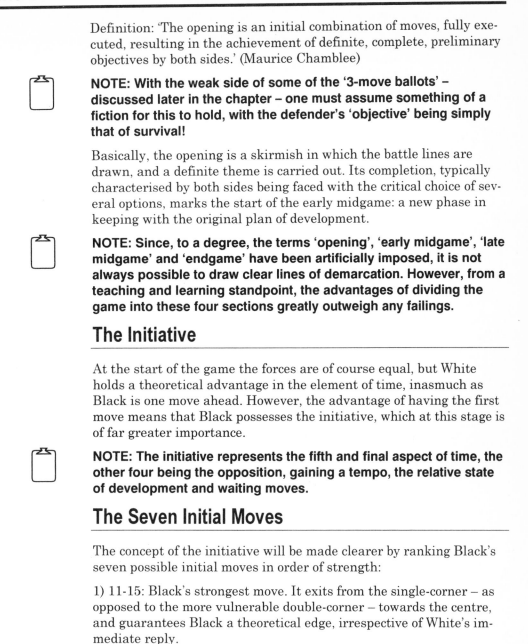

NOTE: With the weak side of some of the '3-move ballots' – discussed later in the chapter – one must assume something of a fiction for this to hold, with the defender's 'objective' being simply that of survival!

Basically, the opening is a skirmish in which the battle lines are drawn, and a definite theme is carried out. Its completion, typically characterised by both sides being faced with the critical choice of several options, marks the start of the early midgame: a new phase in keeping with the original plan of development.

NOTE: Since, to a degree, the terms 'opening', 'early midgame', 'late midgame' and 'endgame' have been artificially imposed, it is not always possible to draw clear lines of demarcation. However, from a teaching and learning standpoint, the advantages of dividing the game into these four sections greatly outweigh any failings.

The Initiative

At the start of the game the forces are of course equal, but White holds a theoretical advantage in the element of time, inasmuch as Black is one move ahead. However, the advantage of having the first move means that Black possesses the initiative, which at this stage is of far greater importance.

NOTE: The initiative represents the fifth and final aspect of time, the other four being the opposition, gaining a tempo, the relative state of development and waiting moves.

The Seven Initial Moves

The concept of the initiative will be made clearer by ranking Black's seven possible initial moves in order of strength:

1) 11-15: Black's strongest move. It exits from the single-corner – as opposed to the more vulnerable double-corner – towards the centre, and guarantees Black a theoretical edge, irrespective of White's immediate reply.

2) 9-14: Again towards the centre, but this time from the double-corner. Consequently, White is able to obtain immediate equality; typically with 22-18, which is the counter-part of 11-15.

3) 11-16: Moving from the single-corner, but this time towards the side, White's reply of 22-18 secures him a slight edge.

4) 10-15: Towards the centre, but from the double-corner, White's response of 21-17 takes advantage of the 'hole' on square 10, giving him the advantage.

5) 10-14: A flanking move which allows White several good replies, of which 24-19 is the strongest.

6) 12-16: Ranks 6th in strength because White can cramp Black's single-corner with the immediate 24-20.

7) 9-13: Black's weakest move (although highly popular with the general public!). It exits from the double-corner to the side, and is powerfully met with 22-18. This ensures White a decided advantage, irrespective of Black's second move.

In other words: 'The strength or weakness of an opening move is measured in terms of the strongest *immediate* reply.' (Maurice Chamblee)

Key Factors In The Opening

The main factors underpinning the entire standard opening developments are:

1) The initiative – try to get it.

2) The centre – seek at least equal shares.

3 The single-corner – develop yours rapidly and be aware of cramps.

4) The double-corner – protect yours and be aware of cramps.

5) Intactness – attempt to disrupt your opponent's position while keeping yours intact.

6) Development – avoid getting ahead in time if possible.

7) Embryonic formations – be alert to them and discard anti-positional moves.

8) Hindsight!

 WARNING: The last factor, which is discussed in more detail in Appendix 2, recognises the limitations of an *entirely* theoretical approach to the game.

Summary

● The term 'opening' refers to a series of moves embracing preliminary objectives.

● The initiative, which plays a prominent role in the opening, is the fifth and final aspect of the element of time.

● Of Black's seven initial moves, 11-15 is the only one which *guarantees* a theoretical edge.

- The strength or weakness of an opening move is measured in terms of the strongest *immediate* reply.

- There are eight factors underpinning all opening developments, of which hindsight is one.

Ballots

GAYP

Up until about 1900, draughts was played almost entirely on the 'Go-As-You-Please' (GAYP) style, where the players had complete freedom of choice in their initial moves. However, an overriding desire to avoid losing, combined with some ill-considered match conditions – encouraging a 'win one and draw the rest' approach – and the universal adoption of 11-15 as a starter, led to the creation, and repetitious playing of, dull drawing variations. Consequently, though in no real sense exhausted – exciting and original matches and tournaments are contested *today* at the highest level – GAYP was dropped as a means of determining the 'heavyweight' championship of the world, and the '2-move restriction' created.

2-Move Restriction

Under the 2-move restriction, which held sway in the USA until 1929 and the British Isles until 1955, the first two moves of the game are randomly 'balloted' from an agreed list of 43; the players playing both sides of the ballot in a sitting for consistency and fairness. Partly for political reasons, partly because standard variations had been established for both sides of all the ballots, and partly because several evenly matched grandmasters had registered long strings of draws against each other, this too was relegated to the sidelines and the '3-move restriction' established.

3-Move Restriction

The main idea behind the new restriction was to increase the number of original games played, and to prevent over-cautious players from relying extensively on memorised analysis. Although preparation and study will, and should (!), always be rewarded, the 3-move restriction, which possesses almost limitless scope, has proved very successful, is going strong today, and is easily the best means of determining the world's finest all-round player (again, both sides of the ballot are always played).

The Complete Deck

There are 302 possible ways in which the first three moves – Black,

White, Black – can be played. Of these, 83 can be eliminated because they are duplicates, and 45 because they result in the loss of a man. This leaves 174 3-move ballots available for consideration, of which 144 are currently deemed suitable for crossboard – over-the-board – play.

 NOTE: The 30 remaining ballots, all thought unsound until now, are being closely scrutinised in postal play. At this stage it appears likely that about 10 of them will receive the stamp of approval, and be added to the deck in the near future.

11-Man Ballot

An esoteric style, this involves the random removal of one man from each side – usually not from the king-rows – in combination with a 2-move ballot. While guaranteeing originality, its artificiality (many positions are reached which could not, even theoretically, be obtained in a GAYP game), its virtual destruction of the literature and its tendency to test brute-force visualisation above all else, while appealing to computer programs and their programmers, has so far proved to be a major stumbling block.

Summary

- There are four different opening conventions: GAYP, 2-move restriction, 3-move restriction and 11-man ballot.

- Although all the conventions have their points, and none are exhausted, the 3-move restriction is universally regarded as the best means of determining the world's finest all-round player.

- 144 3-move ballots are currently accepted as sound for crossboard play, with a further 10 likely to be added in the near future.

- When playing a 3-move ballot, it is vitally important to 'set the scene' by considering the moves you could have played *if you had been given the chance.*

Chapter Seven

Inside the Draughts World

- 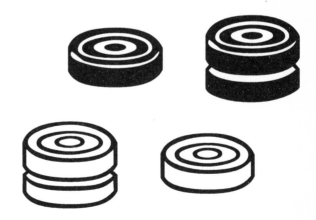 **Computers**

- **Champions**

- **Addresses**

- **Bibliography**

Computers

Easily the two most important draughts-playing computer programs have been those written by Dr Arthur Samuel and Dr Jonathan Schaeffer.

Dr Samuel's program was developed at IBM during the 1960s, and was designed to learn from its mistakes. Although a landmark in its field, it was no champion, managing to achieve, at best, only expert status, and lost heavily in matches contested with the World Champion Walter Hellman and the British Champion Derek Oldbury.

Chinook, on the other hand, which was produced by a team at the University of Alberta with Dr Schaeffer at its head, succeeded, during an active career spanning 1989-1996, in establishing itself as one of the game's greatest ever players. (See *One Jump Ahead* by Dr Schaeffer for a fascinating, and highly personal, account of its successes and failures.) I say one, because, apart from not having had the chance to play the grandmasters of yesteryear, its aggregate results against Asa Long (Chinook won 1 game, lost 1 and drew 18), Don Lafferty (Chinook won 7, lost 8 and drew 109) and, in particular, Dr Marion Tinsley (Chinook won 2, lost 5 and drew 60), were not entirely convincing, particularly against three opponents past their prime, and suggest that it has a mountain to climb before genuine mastery – the correct handling of every legally attainable position – is attained.

More importantly, what Chinook and other, PC-based, programs have done and will do is:

1) To re-demonstrate both the scope of the game (by displaying new attacks and defences) and its profundity (Chinook's 8-piece endgame databases have thrown up a wealth of beautiful examples).

2) To give everyone access to an, ever-willing, world-class opponent (or novice if preferred).

3) To establish, what the empirical evidence has always indicated, that the game has a sound theoretical basis – should always end in a draw – but that it is not susceptible to a formulaic approach. 'Scientific truth says that a properly played game should end in a draw. However, artistic truth tells us it should end in a win, for that player who has the greater creative ability.' (Derek Oldbury)

Champions

The three greatest players of all time are widely regarded as Richard Jordan, Scotland (1872-1911); Samuel Gonotsky, USA (1901-1929) and Dr Marion Tinsley, USA (1927-1995).

The three greatest players of the modern era are universally held to be 1st: Dr Marion Tinsley; 2nd: Walter Hellman, USA (1916-1975) and 3rd: Asa Long, USA (1904-1999). Interestingly, and indicative of the respect accorded the game in some quarters, lengthy obituaries of Derek Oldbury, England, Tinsley and Long have been given in *The Times*, *The Daily Telegraph* and *The Independent* in recent years.

Richard Fortman has been rated the game's leading annotator and commentator for around 50 years. In alphabetical order, he considers the world's current top 20 players to be as follows (USA unless otherwise stated): Karl Albrecht, Ed Bruch, Hugh Burton, Louis Cowie, Paul Davis, Hugh Devlin (Ireland), LaVerne Dibble, Jimmy Grant (Scotland), Richard Hallett, Ron King (Barbados, World Champion), Tim Laverty, Leo Levitt, Elbert Lowder, Jim McCarthy (Ireland), Pat McCarthy (Ireland), Alex Moiseyev Jim Morrison, Richard Pask (England), Tom Watson (Scotland) and Norman Wexler.

Addresses

1) English Draughts Association, formed 1897. Write to EDA Chairman, Mr Ian Caws, 54 Mayfield Road, Ryde, Isle of Wight. PO33 3PR.

2) American Checker Federation, formed 1948. Write to ACF President, Les Balderson, 6517 Patterson Avenue, Richmond, Virginia. 23226 USA.

3) 'World Championship Checkers' PC computer program by Gil Dodgen. Email: Gildodgen@aol.com

4) 'Colossus' PC computer program by Martin Bryant. Email: martinbr@colossus.demon.co.uk

5) 'Sage' PC computer program by Adrian Millett. Email: pcsol@tcp.co.uk

6) 'Nexus' PC computer program by Murray Cash. Email: nexus.suggestions@the nemesis.demon.co.uk

Bibliography

The following 12 works ably complement the material herein, and can be recommended without hesitation. Sadly, like most draughts books, they are only available through specialised dealers, but the official organisations will be happy to put you in touch with them.

Checkers Made Easy by Arthur Reisman. (An introduction)

The Clapham Common Draughts Book by George Trott. (Simple tactics)

Tricks, Traps & Shots by Willie Ryan. (Graded course of tactics arising from games)

Standard Positions by Joe Duffy. (Endgame situations)

Familiar Themes by Ben Boland. (Endgame tactics)

The Wonderful World Of Checkers And Draughts by Tom Wiswell and Jules Leopold. (Problems)

Move Over by Derek Oldbury. (General strategy)

Principles Of Strategy In The Game Of Checkers by Louis Ginsberg (The dyke formation)

Key Formations by Derek Oldbury (Midgame strategy)

Checkers And The Experts by Maurice Chamblee. (Opening strategy)

Key Openings by Richard Pask. (Opening and early midgame database)

International Draughts & Checkers by Derek Oldbury, Dr Marion Tinsley, Tom Wiswell and Professor William Fraser. (Two, deeply annotated, world championship matches)

Chapter Eight

Solutions to Exercises

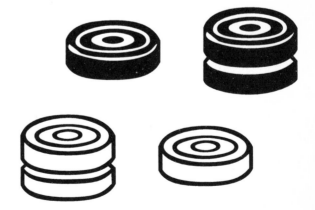

Chapter 3: Solutions

Exercise 1: ... 2-6; 1-10 7-23. White wins.

Exercise 2: ... 10-6; 2-18 15-31. White wins.

Exercise 3: ... 18-15!; 10-19 12-16; 3-12 16-32. White wins.

Exercise 4: ... 15-10!; 6-15 (or 7-14) 27-23; 18-27 25-2. White wins.

Exercise 5: ... 17-14; 9-18 10-6; 3-10 6-31. White wins.

Exercise 6: ... 11-15!; 19-10 28-24; 20-27 32-7. White wins.

Exercise 7: ... 22-18; 13-22 15-10; 6-15 18-11; 8-15 25-11; 5-9 29-25; 9-14 25-22. White wins.

Exercise 8: ... 14-9; 6-13 10-7; 3-10 15-6; 1-10 27-23; 18-27 (or 19-26) 31-6. Drawn.

Exercise 9: ... 21-17; 13-22 30-26; 22-31 24-20; 31-24 20-11!; 8-15 28-1. White wins.

Exercise 10: ... 30-26; 22-31 18-14!; 31-24 14-7; 3-10 28-3. White wins.

Exercise 11: ... 23-19!; 24-15 14-10; 5-14 6-1; 15-6 1-26. White wins.

Exercise 12: ... 17-14; 20-24 (27-31 loses to 26-23) 28-19; 27-23 14-10!; 6-24 26-28. White wins.

Exercise 13: ... 7-2; 18-11 10-7; 3-10 2-6. Drawn.

Exercise 14: ... 24-19; 6-10 (7-11 loses by 19-15) 14-9; 7-11 9-6; 11-15 (10-14 loses by 6-2 and 2-7) 19-16; 10-14 6-10. White wins.

Exercise 15: ... 10-7; 15-24 32-28; 2-11 28-19. White wins.

Exercise 16: ... 15-11; 7-16 24-19; 23-18 19-12; 20-24 17-13; 18-14 12-8; 24-27 8-3. Drawn.

Exercise 17: ... 21-17!; 18-27 19-16!; 12-19 (or 14-21) 2-6; 14-21 6-31. White wins.

Exercise 18: ... 24-19!; 15-24 22-18; 13-22 23-19; 24-15 18-2; 10-15 2-9; 15-19 9-14; 19-23 14-18. White wins.

Exercise 19: ... 21-17; 9-13 10-15!; 19-10 (13-22 loses by 15-24; 22-26 24-19) 18-14; 13-22 14-16. White wins.

Exercise 20: ... 31-26; 23-27 26-22; 25-18 14-32. White wins.

Exercise 21: ... 20-16!; 12-19 14-18!; 5-14 18-20; 19-23 15-18. White wins.

Exercise 22: ... 30-26; 31-22 24-19; 16-23 13-9; 5-14 10-19. White wins.

Exercise 23: ... 26-23; 17-26 18-22; 25-27 32-30. White wins.

Exercise 24: ... 27-24; 22-15 23-19. White wins.

Chapter 4: Solutions

Exercise 1: ... 11-15; 14-17 15-18; 17-21 18-22; 4-8 23-19; 8-12 22-18; 21-25 18-15; 25-30 19-16; 12-19 15-24. White wins.

Exercise 2: ... 12-16; 4-8 16-19; 8-11 19-23; 11-16 23-27; 16-20 27-32; 20-24 30-26; 29-25 26-31; 24-28 31-26. White wins.

Exercise 3: At the moment Black has the opposition. However, White reverses this with ... 10-14; 17-21 16-20; 21-30 20-27; 30-26 14-10. White wins. As in Diagram 12, neither capturing piece was removed from the board, but the opposition was still changed.

Exercise 4: White does not have the opposition, but obtains it in a startling fashion. ... 21-17!!; 13-22 10-15! (10-14 only draws); 18-23 15-18; 22-26 18-27; 26-31 27-24; 31-26 24-19; 26-31 19-15; 31-26 15-18; 26-31 18-22. White wins.

Exercise 5: ... 22-18; 13-17 18-14; 11-15 14-7; 15-24 28-19. White wins.

Exercise 6: ... 31-26; 1-6 26-22; 6-9 22-18; 9-13 18-15; 13-17 11-16!; 3-8 16-12; 8-3 15-11!; 17-22 12-16; 22-26 16-19. White wins.

Exercise 7: ... 10-6!; 2-9 5-1; 23-14 1-5. White wins.

Exercise 8: ... 14-10!; 5-14 6-9. White wins.

Exercise 9: ... 15-11; 20-24 19-15!; 12-19 11-16; 19-23 16-19. White wins.

Exercise 10: ... 31-26; 7-10 27-24!; 20-27 26-23; 10-14 23-19; 15-24 22-8. White wins.

Exercise 11: ... 14-17; 22-25 24-19!; 16-23 31-26; 23-30 17-21; 30-26 21-23. White wins.

Exercise 12: ... 31-26!; 25-30 10-14; 30-23 32-27; 23-32 14-23. White wins.

Exercise 13: ... 16-12; 8-11 19-15; 11-16 30-26!; 22-25 12-8!; 31-22 15-11; 22-15 8-4 (8-3 also wins) 15-8 4-27. White wins.

Exercise 14: ... 19-15!; 10-19 17-14; 19-23 14-5; 6-10 5-1; 23-26 1-6. White wins.

Exercise 15: ... 32-27!; 16-19 27-23!; 19-26 31-22; 20-24 18-15; 10-19 22-18; 24-27 17-14; 27-31 14-5; 6-10 5-1; 31-26 1-6. White wins.

Exercise 16: ... 22-17; 21-25 17-13; 25-30 14-9!; 6-10 3-7; 11-2 9-6; 2-9 13-15. White wins.

Exercise 17: ... 13-17; 18-23 17-22; 16-20 32-27!; 23-32 22-26; 20-27 26-31. White wins.

Exercise 18: ... 6-2; 10-7 8-12!; 7-16 2-7; 4-8 (or 16-20) 12-3. Drawn.

Exercise 19: ... 10-6!; 2-9 8-3; 16-7 3-10; 9-13 10-14. Drawn.

Exercise 20: ... 11-7!; 23-16 3-8; 2-11 8-15; 16-20 15-19. Drawn.

Chapter Nine

Appendices

- 1) The Rules (in detail)
- 2) Understanding the Game
- 3) Glossary

The Rules (in detail)

Draughts Board and Men

1) The draughts board is square in shape and is divided into 64 squares of equal size, alternately light and dark in colour (technically called black and white).

2) The board is arranged between the two players with a black square in the bottom left-hand corner.

3) The game is played on the black squares, which for reference purposes are numbered from 1 to 32.

4) Each player starts with 12 discs, or 'men', all of equal size. One player has dark-coloured men (called Black) and the other has light-coloured men (called White). The colours of the men make a distinct contrast with the colours of the squares of the board.

5) At the start of the game the black men occupy squares 1 to 12, and the white men squares 21 to 32.

Order of Play

6) To start the first game the players decide by the toss of a coin which colour they will have; the winner of the toss choosing colours. In subsequent games the players alternate colours.

7) The first move in each game is made by the player with the black men. Thereafter, the moves are made by each player in turn.

The Moves

8) There are four types of move: the ordinary move of a man, the ordinary move of a king, the jumping move of a man and the jumping move of a king.

Ordinary Move of a Man

9) This is its transfer diagonally forward, left or right, from one square to an immediately neighbouring vacant square.

10) When a man reaches the farthest row forward (the king-row) it becomes a king, and the player's move terminates. The man is crowned by the opponent, who places a man of the same colour on top of it *before making his own move*, borrowing a man from another set if necessary.

Ordinary Move of a King

11) This is its transfer diagonally forward or backward, left or right, from one square to an immediately neighbouring vacant square.

Jumping Move of a Man

12) This is its transfer from one square, over a diagonally adjacent and forward square occupied by an opponent's piece (man or king), on to a vacant square immediately beyond it. On completion of the jump, the jumped piece is removed from the board.

Jumping Move of a King

13) This is similar to that of a man, but may be in a forward or backward direction.

Jumping in General

14) If a jump creates an immediate further jumping opportunity, then the jumping move of the piece is continued until all the jumps are completed. The only exception is that if a man reaches the king-row by means of a jumping move it becomes a king, and the player's move terminates. At the end of the jumping sequence, all jumped pieces are removed from the board in the order in which they were jumped.

15) During a jumping sequence the same piece may only be jumped once.

16) All jumping moves are compulsory, whether offered actively or passively. If there are two or more ways to jump, a player may select any one he wishes; not necessarily that which gains the most pieces.

Touching the Pieces

17) Either player, on intimating his intention to his opponent, is entitled to adjust his own or his opponent's pieces properly on their squares at any time during the game.

18) Unless he has given an adjustment warning, if a player on his turn to move touches a movable piece he must move that piece.

19) If any part of a movable piece is moved over a corner of the square on which it is stationed, the move must be completed in that direction.

False, Improper or Illegal Moves

20) A player making a false, improper or illegal move shall be cautioned for the first offence, and the move recalled. This applies if, for example, a player:

20.1 Omits to jump or to complete a multiple jump.

20.2 On his turn to move, touches a piece which is not movable.

20.3 Moves a piece, either in an ordinary move or a jumping move, on to a wrong square.

20.4 Moves a man backwards.

20.5 When jumping, removes an opponent's piece or pieces which have not been jumped.

20.6 When jumping, removes one or more of his own pieces.

20.7 Continues a jumping move through the king-row with a man.

20.8 Moves a piece when it is not his turn.

21) If any of the pieces are accidentally displaced by the players, or through any cause outside their control, they are replaced without penalty and the game continued.

22) A second false, improper or illegal move during the course of the same game shall result in forfeiture.

23) A player who refuses to adhere to the rules shall immediately forfeit the game.

Result of the Game

24) There are two states to define: the win and the draw.

Definition of a Win

25) The game is won by the player who makes the last move. That is, no move is available to the opponent when it is his turn, either because all his pieces have been captured or his remaining pieces are all blocked.

26) A player also wins if his opponent resigns at any point or forfeits the game by contravening the rules.

Definition of a Draw

27) The game is drawn if, at any stage, both players agree on such a result.

28) 50-move rule. The game shall be declared drawn if a player can demonstrate that both the following conditions hold: neither player has advanced a man towards the king-row during the previous 50 moves; no pieces have been removed from the board during the previous 50 moves. (For the purposes of this rule, a move shall be said to consist of one black move and one white move.)

29) Repetition of position. A draw shall be declared if a player can demonstrate that with his next move he would create the same position for the fourth time during the game.

Understanding the Game

1) The Argument

Writing about Edwin Hunt in the 1936 Long-Hunt World Championship match book, Ben Carson stated: '[For Hunt] there is no laborious memory work necessary, it appears, because he understands the mechanism of the formations so perfectly, appreciating the why of every move.' I was 17 when I read this for the first time – in 1979, not 1936! – and Carson's comment has intrigued me ever since. Is it really possible to *understand*, find a valid reason for, every move played? After 21 years of close study my verdict is a qualified Yes. Hopefully, an explanation of my reasons will give you a greater insight into the nature of the game; particularly as played at the highest level.

2) Popular Perceptions

Many of the books on draughts, especially the older ones, consist of page after page of dry columns of numbers, without any explanation given as to the motives behind the moves. This has, understandably, given rise to the erroneous impression that the game is primarily a memory test, and that strategy has a negligible role to play. The situation is further hindered by cringe-making statements such as the following: 'As to general advice relative to draughts-playing, next to nothing can be learnt from a volume of such instruction.' (George Walker's Edition of Sturges' Guide) Thanks for nothing! Ask any strong player for his view, however, and you get a totally different perspective:

1) 'The game of checkers is fundamentally a test of what you can see, rather than what you can remember.' (Dr Marion Tinsley)

2) 'A lively and disciplined imagination, coupled with ability, ambition, judgement, confidence, generalship, patience, knowledge, visualisation, memory, precision and finesse are the qualities needed to lead one to the coveted realm of the immortal checker master.' (Tom Wiswell)

3) 'If you have an imagination, know the truth when you see it, and can keep a straight face, then you are half-way [to becoming a draughts champion].' (Derek Oldbury)

In order to focus the argument, and make sense of the gulf which exists between myth and reality, it is necessary to look separately at the two types of position you can find yourself in: one where you are on unfamiliar ground; one where you are on familiar ground.

3) Unfamiliar Positions

During Chinook's development, Dr Jonathan Schaeffer found it '...amazing how strong a game of checkers a program can play with very little knowledge.' His view is substantiated when you play a game against a PC-based program and turn off the book facility: it may lose occasionally, after a hard fight, but always plays to a high standard. This parallels human experience: a player with only minimal book knowledge, but possessed of good judgement and well-developed powers of visualisation, can pick out a perfectly playable move across the board a high percentage of the time. Significantly, almost all the greats of the game achieved notable successes before they were 21, often against players of 20 or 30 years' experience. Therefore, unless you have grandmasterly ambitions, refining your judgement and enhancing your visualisation by playing hard, regular practice games, preferably under the tournament time limit of 30 moves per hour, against worthy opponents, including computers, is sufficient.

Why then have authors been so reluctant to talk in general terms? The answer, I suspect, lies with the unreasonable expectations of the critics. Landmark works such as Ginsberg's *Principles Of Strategy In The Game Of Checkers*, Chamblee's *Checkers And The Experts* and Oldbury's *Move Over* have been unfairly criticised when apparent 'exceptions' were found to their 'rules'. In fact, none of these authors claimed to have discovered an infallible 'system', but merely argued that an adoption of their methods, *in tandem with all the other requisites*, would lead to a significantly improved standard of play.

In short, while it is universally accepted that the game is not susceptible to a strictly mathematical approach, at least not to one which would be of any value to a human being, it is a giant, and illogical, leap to infer that, therefore, all strategic thinking is valueless. 'Looking ahead' blindly in all directions, trying to find something tactical to chew on, is the only alternative, and it assuredly doesn't work! 'Serviceable playing hints', as Arthur Reisman so aptly described them, are essential. The fear of being labelled a crank, and the time and effort required to produce lucid, coherent advice, has thus led many writers to play safe; remaining mute and leaving the moves to speak for themselves. (Of course, I concede that if you could look ahead far enough, then strategy would indeed become superfluous!)

4) Familiar Positions

Understanding 'book' games is an entirely different issue, and is largely a study in chronology. In the game's infancy, in the absence of books, the players were forced to rely on their own judgement. Most of the time, the logical, or natural move stood up well, but occasionally it was found to be unsatisfactory – leading to undesirable complications, say, or even a loss – and an alternative was sought. Likewise, with computer programs, no matter how highly-tuned the evaluation function, programmers discovered that the depth and profundity of the game would always throw up exceptions (strictly speaking there are no rules, and therefore no exceptions). Hence the value of knowledge: *all other factors being equal*, a player armed with some of these exceptions will hold the edge over one who isn't. Unfortunately, far from being a collection of high quality games and analysis, 'published play' is a haphazard mixture of good and bad, 90% of which is unsound or obsolete. Since it's only worth studying material which is authentic, reliable and relevant – 'It's not the lines you know, but the *relevant* lines you know that counts.' (Don Lafferty) – you should, if you are ambitious, initially limit yourself to the tried and tested content of books such as *Basic Checkers* by Richard Fortman and *Solid Checkers* by myself, which are based almost entirely upon high quality matches and tournaments.

Then, assuming you have a good measure of understanding – it's impossible otherwise! – you should play through the book games, applying strategic principles and look-ahead to each move, in an endeavour to identify the exceptions; essentially those falling outside your range of candidate moves. (Chinook's minimal 'anti-book' was restricted to natural *losses*.) Particularly in the case of the lop-sided ballots, your attention should be given to the defence, which is, unquestionably, the key to understanding the attack. In each case, the specific reason for an exception should be hunted-out. It may be because of the move's restrictive qualities, because it avoids complications, because it transposes, possibly at some cost, into known territory, because, as part of a combination, it represents the only way to beat a losing move – and it's worth noting that, in draughts, when you miss a win, *the advantage swings inexorably to your opponent* – or, in a few cases, simply because every other move has been shown to lose!

Identifying these exceptions, or key moves, and the reasons behind them, together with the specific formation, tactics, theme, transition, holds, landing, motifs etc. involved – some of which are beyond the scope of this book – will enable you to later *reconstruct* the game with a minimum of rote memory. (In fact, you should 'cut-off' the game at the point where you are confident you can handle it on your own: memorising entire variations which can, in part or in whole, be handled perfectly well crossboard is both time-wasting and inhibiting.) Moreover, in the heat of battle, reconstructing, as opposed to mere recalling, is much safer, more sensitive to move order changes by the opponent, and more likely to result in consistency when, at some point, you are thrown on your own resources. 'When a grandmaster plays, you can't see the joins.' (Pat McCarthy)

5) The Next Step

Finally, if you are an aspiring grandmaster, you will tailor the standard material to your own needs, thereby defining an individual style and, having a broad idea of what is generally known and possibly with the assistance of a computer, *create original attacks and defences* – known as 'cooks' in the trade.

Glossary

A[attacking]-Lines: The two double-corner diagonals stretching from 32 to 5 and 1 to 28.

Backward Men: Men which have made little progress towards the opponent's king-row. They often prove a liability in the endgame, and when held fast by the opponent, are known as pivot men.

Bridge: A configuration consisting of white men on 30 and 32, and a black man on 23. (1, 3 and 10.)

Centre: Squares 14, 15, 18 and 19.

Classics: Recurring late midgame positions of great importance. The four major classics are Fifth Position, Lucas' Position, Cowan's Coup and Strickland's Draw.

Crossboard: 1) To play over-the-board, as opposed to analysing or playing by correspondence. 2) To be in an unfamiliar position. That is, to play from 'your head' rather than from 'the book'.

D[defensive]-Line: The single-corner diagonal stretching from 29 to 4.

Dog-Holes: Squares 5(White) and 28(Black). Generally to be avoided because of their poor mobility.

Double-Corner: In White's case, squares 24, 27, 28 and 32; in Black's case squares 1, 5, 6 and 9.

Double-Corner Cramp: A restriction of mobility of the men in this region of the board.

Dust-Holes: Squares 12(White) and 21(Black). Generally to be avoided because of their poor mobility.

E[equality]-Lines: The two diagonals stretching from 30 to 12 and 3 to 21.

Early Midgame: Probably the most important phase of the game, leading from the opening up to a climactic point signifying the start of the late midgame.

Elbow: A configuration consisting of black men (say) on 6, 10 and 14. It is often vulnerable to attack.

Elementary Tactical Devices: Usually simple ways of gaining a piece, featuring the 2 For 1, 2 For 2, 3 For 2, Rebound, In-And-Out, Double-Corner Devices, Breeches, Fork and Optional Jumps.

Elimination: The process of deciding upon a move by eliminating those which are unsatisfactory.

Endgame: A game ending, in which both sides have achieved a king; or at least have gained a clear run to the king-row (the final row of the board). The two most important endgames are First Position and Second Position, both of which are actually *situations* embracing thousands of *positions*.

FORCE: Intimately associated with tactics, this is one of three key elements operating in the game.

Formations: Midgame structures consisting of six or more men. The six major formations are the Dyke (Long and Short), Pyramid, Phalanx, Mill, Echelon and Mixed.

Late Midgame: This leads from the conclusion of the early midgame to the, possible, start of the endgame.

Opening: An initial combination of moves, resulting in the completion of preliminary objectives.

Opposition: The ability to check the advance of opposing pieces beyond a certain point.

Pitch: The sacrifice of a piece, often on positional grounds. Widely known as 'the soul of draughts'.

Problem: A composed study in the element of force.

Single-Corner: In White's case, squares 21, 22, 25 and 29; in Black's case squares 4, 8, 11 and 12.

Single-Corner Cramp: A restriction of mobility of the men in this region of the board.

SPACE: Intimately associated with mobility – freedom of movement – this is one of three key elements operating in the game, and is mainly to do with the construction/maintenance of formations.

Strategy: Long-term planning.

Tactics: The various 'tricks of the trade' used to carry out a strategic plan. They can be very complex!

Themes: Essentially endgame tactics. The thirteen major themes are Self-Destruct, Changing Guard, Vice, Pocket, Hanging Man, Single-Corner Block, Double-Corner Block, Squeeze, Steal, Nipped At The Wire, Captive Cossacks, Ace In The Hole and Hobson's Choice.

TIME: One of three key elements operating in the game. It is multi-faceted, consisting of the opposition, gaining a tempo, the relative state of development, waiting moves and the initiative.

Visualisation: Moving the pieces around in your mind's eye. Also referred to as looking ahead.